medicine for a sick world

medicine for a sick world

essays and reflections

DAVID LEFKOWITZ

INTRODUCTION BY LEVI A. OLAN

PREFACE BY UMPHREY LEE

DALLAS

SOUTHERN METHODIST UNIVERSITY PRESS

1952

WITH DEVOTION
FOR MY WIFE
OF FIFTY YEARS

PREFACE

It is an honor to be asked to write the preface to this book of essays and sermons by Doctor David Lefkowitz, Rabbi Emeritus of Temple Emanu-El.

There are both personal and professional reasons for my pleasure in writing these brief words. Three years after Doctor Lefkowitz came to Dallas to be the rabbi of Temple Emanu-El, I came to the city to be the pastor of a Methodist Church. For nearly thirty years we have been associated in various ways, particularly in connection with Southern Methodist University. I can testify out of this more than a quarter of a century of personal knowledge and of association with Doctor Lefkowitz to his stature as a spiritual leader.

Very fittingly, this volume is published by the Southern Methodist University Press. The essays and sermons are of a quality that would do honor to any university. They give an insight into the best thinking of the liberal Jewish community in this country and they have independent value for their moral and spiritual qualities.

Nearly two and a half decades ago this University conferred an honorary degree on Doctor Lefkowitz, and this book is only an added justification for that degree.

UMPHREY LEE

Southern Methodist University
Dallas, Texas
February 29, 1952

vii

CONTENTS

Preface   **vii**

Introduction   **xi**

ESSAYS

The American Principle of the Separation
    of Church and State   1

The Relation of the Life and Philosophy
    of Spinoza to Judaism   27

The Primacy of the Synagogue:
    How Can It Be Re-established?   45

The Need of a New Idealism   62

Goethe at Aspen, Colorado, and His Disciples   71

SERMONS

Medicine for a Sick World   91

The Quest of the Ages   98

Standing in the Way: Rest for the Soul   105

Is Science Enough?   111

The Hardened Heart or the Serene Soul — Which?   118

Where is Thy God?   125

The Voice of God Is Calling   132

God Spoke Amid the Tumult of the World   139

False Gods: The Golden Calf and Others   145

The Religion of Thinking Men   152

Prayer — the Voice of Religion   159

Home, the Bulwark of Civilization   166

Realities and Shams of Success   172

The Gift of Memory for These Times   179

Treasures Discarded   185

Thankfulness — the Fine Fruit
    of Great Cultivation   193

At the Crossroads: Three Questions, One Answer   200

Two Historic Refusals   206

The Flood, Dove, and Rainbow — and
    Another Bystander   212

Two Voices — To Which Shall We Listen?   218

The Submerged Cathedral   224

Why I Am a Jew   232

INTRODUCTION

The twentieth century dawned upon the horizon, full of confidence and hope for man's future. Science had reduced the universe to the simple formula of matter plus law, which had about it a common-sense appeal to the practical-minded of the race. The story of creation was supplanted by the theory of evolution, which operated in accordance with known laws of struggle and adaptation. Psychology was turning mind into a brain whose functions were controlled by the fixed laws of physiology and chemistry. Intellectually, life was a neat little package of matter subject to mechanical laws. All that men needed for the perfect life was to discover the rules that fitted matter.

The social prospects were the brightest since the Pax Romana. War at its worst was limited to a skirmish in a fixed corner of the world. Britannia ruled the waves and gave stolidity to the universe. When the Spanish sank the *Maine* America flexed its growing muscles and indicated that it would not endure oppressive imperialism near its shores. Germany had not yet felt the urge to expand its place in history, and Russia was asleep with only a half-cocked eye toward Japan. The prospect for peace among nations was never better.

The American scene was the most promising in an age of unlimited promises. Enterprising men were joining initiative, shrewdness, and the natural resources of the land to create the beginnings of a giant industrial machine. Millions of Europeans flocked to America's shores in the hope of finding freedom and prosperity. The gates were wide open and the peoples couldn't get in fast enough. They crowded into great urban centers, where mills and factories were rising with phenomenal speed. There was work for all who wanted it, and citizenship with its privileges was assured to any who sought it. The populace was a rough and unformed mass, but it was hopeful and self-assured. There was only one faith which united all men, the belief that progress was as inevitable as the rising of the sun each day. It would have taken a prophet of the stature of Amos to predict what the next half-century had in store for humankind.

It was in this year of unbounded hope, in June, 1900, that the president of the Hebrew Union College in Cincinnati, Rabbi Isaac Mayer Wise, laid his hands in the traditional manner upon the head of David Lefkowitz and ordained him a rabbi, a teacher of God unto men. Wise, himself, had left Bohemia in the fifties because he needed room for his free spirit and his humanitarian faith. In America, he beheld the promised land where people of many backgrounds and varying creeds could build a society long ago envisioned by the Hebrew prophets. The country was free of the old world traditions and prejudices: it gave promise of responding to liberal ideas and social ideals. He saw the opportunity here for his Jewish faith to express its prophetic hope of justice and righteousness while throwing off some of the old and meaningless accretions of custom and form which the centuries had hardened and preserved. In this year which ushered in the twentieth century, the promise of this faith seemed fulfilled. The young ordained rabbi was setting out in an atmosphere of confidence and trust in the liberal progress of his generation.

He was twenty-five years old as he stood before the ark to accept the blessing of his teacher. What had brought him there in the first place? In a land so full of opportunities for worldly success, why should a young man choose to devote his life to a career which at best is unrewarding in material goods? The answer to this searching question must, it seems, remain locked in the mystery of our human natures. Why men choose a profession of service instead of worldly gain has never been satisfactorily explained, not even by modern psychologists. The statistics of his life may give a partial answer, but the more deciding factor will elude us.

David Lefkowitz was born on April 11, 1875, in Eperies, Austria-Hungary, the sixth child of Benjamin and Lena Lefkowitz. His father died in 1879 after being rescued from shipwreck while emigrating to the United States. His oldest brother, educated at the University of Budapest, became a physician, and remained in Austria-Hungary; he died there while fighting in the army in 1918. Another brother and sister emigrated to the United States in 1879, and the mother took her three remaining children and joined them in New York City in 1881.

The saga of the immigrant boy who makes the most of American opportunity and freedom has been recounted many times. But we are concerned here not with the usual story of success. Our unique story is of a young man who chose to exploit the resources of America for service in the field of moral and spiritual values. To what shall we attribute this choice? If a hard and trying childhood is the answer, it can be found here. The mother could not maintain her children in this new land, and David, along with his younger brother, entered the Hebrew Orphan Asylum in New York City. Here he remained throughout his public school years and five years while attending the College of the City of New York. Two of these later years were spent in the additional work of being a governor of the orphan asylum under the superintendent. The major interest of the young man during these years was art, to the extent that in the summer of 1896 he matriculated at the Art Students League.

What turned a young man from a career as an artist to service in the ministry? Is there a logical and spiritual relationship between art and religion? It is true that at the asylum there were special courses in Jewish history, Hebrew grammar and Bible and Talmud, taught by renowned scholars. Is this where the answer may be found? Was it that Dr. Gotthard Deutsch, historian and teacher at the Hebrew Union College, talked with the young man? Dr. Deutsch was one of the most attractive personalities of his day, and no student who ever came before him failed to feel the touch of his great and rich personality. Suffice it to say that in the fall of 1896 young Lefkowitz entered the seminary in Cincinnati, and in June, 1900, was ordained rabbi and teacher. If we are puzzled by his choice of the rabbinate as a life calling, the answer is given in the next fifty years of a devoted and consecrated ministry.

What are the influences that mold the character of a man's work? Do the years in the orphan home have a special significance? Was the German teacher, Dr. Herman Baar, superintendent of the home, with his military discipline, his precise sermons, his knowledge of Hebrew and Jewish religious lore, a major factor? Was it Dr. Johnson of the College of the City of New York, who lectured on the history of philosophy, or Dr. Doremus, who taught science? Let it be noted that the degree attained was the Bachelor of Science. At the University of Cincinnati, which the young man attended while studying at the Hebrew Union College, Dr. Benedict introduced him to the philosophy of German idealism. Perhaps the major influence, however, was in the person of Dr. Wise, who represented a reasoned religious outlook as opposed to the worship of tradition as such. His humane attitude, opposing the stuffed-shirt and calling upon the young rabbi to live on the level of his people, certainly had great weight in the future years of service.

It is a vain and fruitless search to try to unearth the forces that mold the man. Surely, a major place must be given to Sadie Braham, whom the young rabbi married on October 10, 1901. She became "Aunt Sadie" to thousands of people as she took her place in the community. Her work of half a century with the Visiting Nurses Association, over which she presided at one time, gives us a clue to her interests. Her rearing of four children amidst a full course of service to congregational work and community enterprise is an indication of her energy and devotion. Her active participation in religious life as choir leader, as organizer and president of the Sisterhood of the Temple, as a director of National Federation of Temple Sisterhoods — all of these are signs of her immeasurable influence. In the final analysis, a man is born with a gift from God and all the influences around him merely strengthen and quicken his talents. All is not environment and heredity — there is a divine blessing which man gets hold of and fulfils.

At the turn of the century Dayton, Ohio, was an average midwestern community which lay between the capital city of Columbus and the Queen City of Cincinnati. It was a steady, moderately progressive American city with no special faults or virtues. To the Reform Congregation, Bene Jeshurun, counting eighty-two families, Rabbi David Lefkowitz was called for his first charge. He was to remain here for twenty years and leave behind him a congregation of over three hundred families. The temper and purpose of the man soon found natural expression.

Religion embodies within itself two major traditions, the priestly and the prophetic. The first deals with the institution of faith, the second with its application to the lives of men. Though he did not neglect the vital role of worship, teaching, and pastoral care, the needs of human life stirred the young rabbi into a course which was to be his major achievement. The function of a teacher is to serve men where they need help most urgently. Thus we find that he soon became president of the Humane Society, leader in the movement of the Playground and Garden Association, and the first chairman and local organizer of the American Red Cross. In 1913 the city of Dayton suffered the horrors of one of the worst floods in American history. Some day, the story of the role played by David Lefkowitz should be told in full. Suffice it here to note that he supervised the health and feeding of one of the four sections of the city.

It was not all a simple program of social service for the community as a whole. The prophetic tradition is rooted in morality, and evil disturbs a religious teacher. Thus the rabbi was appointed chairman of a Committee of Investigation to delve into the corruption which was besmirching the official municipal government. He cleaned it all out, but not without a show of courage the story of which reads like a mystery thriller. At one point he was called and told by a friend not to leave his house to attend divine services, because the corrupt political machine was out to get him. Then there was the attempt to introduce Bible reading in the public schools, a program that threatened the cherished idea of the separation of church and state. The prophetic indignation again manifested itself and the rabbi organized protest meetings and wrote in clear and direct phrases about the danger of such a move. His booklet on the subject became a national sourcebook for all who aimed to keep the religious issue out of the public school. It was this struggle, too, that brought him the appointment to the first chairmanship of the Committee of Church and State of the Central Conference of American Rabbis.

The direction of his ministry became clearer as the years passed by; it was one of service to all men regardless of creed, color, or station in life. Nothing human was alien to a teacher of the faith of God. Thus, he preached in churches of all denominations and was so highly regarded by the YMCA that he was urged to go overseas during World War I to help straighten out that Christian agency in its war work at the front. When he decided finally to accept another call, it was a distinguished body of citizens of all faiths who framed a petition requesting that he remain as rabbi, and they backed their petition with an offer to help support any program which might be involved.

Why, at the height of his usefulness to the congregation and to the community, did the rabbi accept the invitation to become rabbi of Temple Emanu-El of Dallas, Texas? There was not the incentive of financial advantage, for the people of Dayton, both Jewish and Christian, were prepared to do more than the just measure. In 1920 the membership of the Texas congregation was actually smaller than that of the one in Dayton. A rabbi with the position and influence of David Lefkowitz could have rolled along easily and comfortably for the rest of his life. Why should a man begin all over again among new people and with a whole set of new problems? Essentially, the time had come in his ministry when his vision for a dynamic Jewish religious program called for facilities which could house and foster an expanded congregational life. In Dallas, he saw both the building and the human possibilities. It fired his imagination, and amidst great regret and many tears he moved his family and his religious fervor to this new and promising city of the Southwest.

Dallas in 1920 revealed the potentialities of the great city it was to become. Being the financial center of the oil, cattle, and cotton trade of its region, it had attracted many enterprising people and was rapidly attaining metropolitan stature. The arts and the sciences were encouraged by citizens who sensed the cultural needs of a modern, growing community. In this setting, the mature talents of Temple Emanu-El's new rabbi were to find their richest fulfilment. It was natural for him to enter immediately upon a course of community service, serving on the Board of the Associated Charities, the Family Service, and being chairman of the Red Cross chapter. A list of his civic endeavors — much too long to be recorded here — would only point up the deep concern he has had for the needs of citizens in their social and cultural lives.

His major achievement in Dallas has been the building of a congregation which numbered just over two hundred families when he arrived to more than a thousand when he retired on January 1, 1949. Given adequate facilities, he set in motion a program of religious education which reflected the faith of his fathers. Invited in his first year to present a religious program over the radio, he created one of the most forceful pulpits of the air, from which his liberal religious message reached out to untold thousands of listeners and admirers. The Jewish community found in him a ready helper and guide. Thus, he helped create the Jewish Welfare Federation, and the southwestern Chautauqua where the religious school teachers of the region met to improve the methods and goals of their educational work. He helped found the Texas Kallah of Rabbis and was its president and chancellor. At its meetings he read scholarly papers to his fellow-rabbis. By 1930 his stature was such that his colleagues elected him president of the Central Conference of American Rabbis, and he then became vice-president of the World Union of Progressive Judaism. In 1933 his alma mater conferred upon him the honorary degree of

Doctor of Divinity which was the logical recognition for the status he had achieved.

Let no one assume that this was a journey unimpeded by serious problems and challenging obstacles. One year after his arrival in Dallas, the new rabbi was face to face with the most severe challenge to his ideals and faith. The community was in the throes of a violent conflict between hooded men of prejudice and the forces of brotherhood. The atmosphere was tense and charged with danger, and cautious men skirted the issue. But a descendant of the prophets has no choice. The rabbi became one of the leading forces in the battle against prejudice. He was joined by citizens of all faiths, and together they ultimately averted the threat. A full-length biography of Rabbi Lefkowitz should some day relate the whole story of this courageous and inspired episode. From this episode came new associations with other liberal spirits and his relationship with the Critic Club of Dallas, composed of some of the more thoughtful citizens who met to think with each other on matters of mind and faith. In 1935 the rabbi was raised to the Thirty-Third Degree Honorary, by the Scottish Rite of Masonry.

The relationship of Rabbi Lefkowitz to Southern Methodist University deserves separate and full treatment. This university, today one of the renowned institutions of higher learning, is controlled by a board appointed by the Methodist church, whose vision is a direct expression of the faith of that church. In 1928, only eight years after his arrival in Dallas, Rabbi Lefkowitz received the honorary degree of LL.D. from S.M.U. He preached frequently in the university chapel. Upon his retirement in 1949 from the active rabbinate of the Temple, he was appointed visiting professor at the Perkins School of Theology of the university, lecturing on contemporary Judaism. To climax this unusual relationship, the congregation of Temple Emanu-El, in honor of the fiftieth wedding anniversary of the rabbi and his wife, established in 1951 the Sadie and David Lefkowitz Collection of Judaica at the Bridwell Library of the theology school.

Thus far, this has been an account of a few of the tangible and visible activities of a devoted religious teacher. Impressive as the record is, it is but a fraction of the whole, and it is set down only in order to help the reader of this volume to understand the spirit of the author. What is not set down, and perhaps never can be reduced to words, is the man himself. His supreme gift is his quiet but firm personality with its full range from pure sympathy and smiling friendliness toward all creatures to, on occasion, sternly righteous indignation. The most influential achievement of Dr. Lefkowitz is written in the lives of thousands of people to whom he has ministered in times of heartbreak and joy, in hours of frustration and loss, in perplexities and despair. This ministry of his sensitive spirit to the spiritual needs of all whom he has touched must remain a document written in life and never captured on paper. If now we ask ourselves why this young man chose a religious ministry instead of a career in art or the professions, or business, the answer is, perhaps, found in the revelation that God had given him a talent to serve men and strengthened his will to fulfil his blessed gift.

A half-century has elapsed since the young, newly ordained rabbi set out into a world full of confidence in the steady forward march of progress. The faith that characterized the turn of this century rings hollow to the ears of many in our day. There have been two World Wars of frightening proportions, and the prospect of an even greater and more terrifying conflict holds all the world in its grip. Science has crowned its achievement with the invention of an atomic bomb which threatens our whole civilization. Industrial progress in America has brought prosperity and a high standard of living, but it has also sharpened and extended the conflict of capital and labor. The hooded men of prejudice in America, temporarily overshadowed in vicious bigotry by naziism with its human crematories, still sometimes find listeners for their message of hate. The hour is symbolized by the ominousness of a big cold war and the agony of a little live war. Who was prophet enough in June of 1900 to have predicted the events of this half-century?

Men have turned to many nostrums in these years in the attempt to cure the ills of the age. Some have taken refuge in the cult of the irrational, and renouncing reason and science have turned to a philosophy which escapes reality by a flight into the unknown. Some have allied themselves with political and social movements whose platforms promise a panacea for all man's ills. Some have adopted the new psychology and look for the day when the world will be healed by the new doctors of the mind and emotions. Through all this, the ranks of the liberals who were the hope of the world at the beginning of this century have thinned out.

David Lefkowitz, however, has remained the genuine liberal through this entire period. His faith is rooted in the belief that there is God in history and in mankind. Human nature, for him, has the potentiality of revealing its goodness and godliness. The trouble with the world is the failure of men to realize their best, not the inadequacy of a political or social formula. It is men becoming conscious of their spiritual nature who will build the world of peace and concord. This basic faith has not been shaken in all of these troubled and fearful years. In the concluding pages of his paper on Goethe, read to the Critic Club fifty years after his ordination, and now published in this volume, Rabbi Lefkowitz restated his faith.

Having tried every course in life to achieve meaning, Dr. Faustus returns to the little island to do his best there. In that sense, too, David Lefkowitz has labored in the little island around himself to give men the realization of their spiritual dignity and their moral potential. To a sick world, the pages of this volume bring a medicine tried and tested over a half-century of consecrated service. But what is more, it is the medicine which religion at its best has always had in store for men when they are sick.

LEVI A. OLAN

Dallas, Texas,
January 15, 1952.

ESSAYS

THE AMERICAN PRINCIPLE OF THE
SEPARATION OF CHURCH AND STATE

I N THE COURSE of debate during the memorable Virginia Constitutional Convention of 1776, one of the speakers said, "There can be no liberty without frequent recurrence to fundamental principles." It is certainly true that custom stales the freshness of great liberties won at high cost; that our tired vision draws narrow horizons, whereas in the heat of a revolt against injustice no bounds or limitations on justice were noted or would have been tolerated. One of the perils most to be feared in the high adventure of translating moral principles into political practice is the jaded spirit after the victory, the tarnishing and dulling of the bright treasure through the handling and habitude of the years. For that reason, even liberty and all its implications need a frequent recurrence to fundamental principles. As events from time to time in the course of our nation's political history have shown, our American liberties as embodied in a hundred safeguards are apt to be narrowly construed, or even misconstrued, and the pristine enthusiasm for them sadly dimmed, unless now and then we turn back to the day when they were wonderfully new and were announced with the glowing conviction and victorious voice of a divine revelation. To recapture that faith in the principles of our American liberties should be the object of frequent recurrence to the days when they were being forged on the anvil of history.

One of those principles, one of the foremost of them,

Paper read before the Central Conference of American Rabbis, Cincinnati, Ohio, June, 1932.

1

is the separation of church and state. David Dudley Field, great jurist and student of international law, said in describing "American Progress in Jurisprudence":

The greatest achievement ever made in the cause of human progress is the total and final separation of church and state. If we had nothing else to boast of, we could lay claim with justice that first among the nations we of this country made it an article of organic law that the relations between man and his Maker were a private concern, into which other men have no right to intrude. To measure the stride thus made for the Emancipation of the race, we have only to look back over the centuries that have gone before us, and recall the dreadful persecutions in the name of religion that have filled the world.

Another great jurist of our own faith, Judge Irving Lehman of the Court of Appeals of New York, speaks of this principle of freedom of thought and conscience as "perhaps the greatest contribution which America has made to political thought and ideals and practice." To realize that this principle needs reburnishing in our day by recurrence to the thoughts and acts and passions out of which it was flamingly fashioned, we need only refer to American history of the last two or three lustrums. Besides the Ku Klux Klan, which, though largely concerned with a racial and political controversy, had in it a very definite element of religious intolerance, we can note frequent attempts to sectarianize our central and state governments as well as our public schools.

And it is certainly with a singular and felicitous appropriateness that this recurrence to first principles in the matter of separation of church and state has been made by the Central Conference of American Rabbis a part of our American tribute to George Washington on the occasion of the bicentenary celebration of his birth. For Washington, with the other great leaders of thought and action in the Revolution, such as Franklin, Jefferson, and Madison, was a man of splendid liberality of mind and spirit who was convinced that thought and conscience cannot be constrained and that civil government may not enter into realms where constraint is both undesirable and impossible. He was one of those who in the day of the formation of our Constitution saw that freedom of thought is a matter of right and not of favor, and he helped to embody that principle in the fundamental law of our country.

Washington's conception of toleration was surprisingly enlightened. In his letter to the Hebrew Congregation of the City of Savannah, dated May 19, 1790, he rejoices "that a spirit of liberty and philanthropy is much more prevalent than it formerly was among the enlightened nations of the earth," and hopes that the Jewish people "will benefit thereby in proportion as it shall become still more extensive." And he adds:

Happily, the people of the United States of America have, in many instances, exhibited examples worthy of imitation, the salutary influence of which will doubtless extend much farther, if gratefully enjoying those blessings of peace, which under the favor of heaven have been obtained by fortitude in war, they shall conduct themselves with reverence to the Deity, and with charity toward their fellow-creatures.

Again, he leaves no doubt as to his attitude toward the inherent human rights of all men when in his significant letter to the Hebrew Congregation in Newport, Rhode Island, he writes:

The Citizens of the United States of America have a right to applaud themselves for having given to mankind examples of an enlarged and liberal policy; a policy worthy of imitation. All possess alike liberty of conscience and immunities of citizenship. It is now no more that toleration is spoken of, as if it was by the indulgence of one class of people, that another enjoyed the exercise of their inherent natural rights. For happily the Government of the United States, which gives to

3

bigotry no sanction, to persecution no assistance, requires only that they who live under its protection should demean themselves as good citizens, in giving it on all occasions their effectual support.

To the Bishops of the Methodist Episcopal Church in the United States he wrote in May, 1789, "It shall still be my endeavor to manifest, by overt acts, the purity of my inclinations for promoting the happiness of mankind, as well as the sincerity of my desires to contribute whatever may be in my power towards the preservation of the civil and religious liberties of the American people." In the same month and year, he wrote to the General Committee Representing the United Baptist Churches of Virginia:

If I could have entertained the slightest apprehension, that the constitution framed in the convention, where I had the honor to preside, might possibly endanger the religious rights of any ecclesiastical society, certainly I would never have placed my signature to it; and, if I could now conceive that the general government might ever be so administered as to render the liberty of conscience insecure, I beg you will be persuaded, that no one would be more zealous than myself to establish effectual barriers against the horrors of spiritual tyranny, and every species of religious persecution. For you doubtless remember, that I have often expressed my sentiments, that every man, conducting himself as a good citizen, and being accountable to God alone for his religious opinions, ought to be protected in worshipping the Deity according to the dictates of his own conscience.

In a letter to Sir Edward Newenham, written October 20, 1792, Washington says, "Of all the animosities which have existed among mankind, those which are caused by a difference of sentiments in religion . . . ought most to be deprecated." In December, 1789, he optimistically addressed to the Roman Catholics in the United States the sentiment that "as mankind become more liberal, they will be more apt to allow, that all those, who conduct themselves as worthy members of the community, are equally entitled to the protection of civil government. I hope ever to see America among the foremost nations in examples of justice and liberality." To the General Assembly of the Presbyterian Church in the United States, he writes in a letter of May, 1789: "While all men within our territories are protected in worshipping the Deity according to the dictates of their consciences, it is rationally to be expected from them in return that they will all be emulous of evincing the sanctity of their professions by the innocence of their lives and the beneficence of their actions."

Though he was fundamentally opposed to any restraint of religious principles, Washington yet hesitated to go the full length in discountenancing assessments by the state for the support of religious establishments, as may be seen from his letter to George Mason, October 3, 1785, in which he says:

Although no man's sentiments are more opposed to any kind of restraint upon religious principles than mine are, yet, I must confess, that I am not amongst the number of those, who are so much alarmed at the thought of making people pay toward the support of that which they profess, if of the denomination of Christians, or declare themselves Jews, Mahometans, or otherwise, and thereby obtain proper relief. As the matter now stands, I wish an assessment had never been agitated, and as it has gone so far, that the bill [Assessment Bill] could die an easy death.

Perhaps it should be stated in this connection that the law in Virginia as finally passed, no doubt with Washington's assistance, certainly with his sympathy, was:

That no man shall be compelled to frequent or support any religious worship, place or ministry whatsoever, nor shall be

5

enforced, restrained, molested, or otherwise suffer on account of his religious opinions or belief; but that all men shall be free to possess, and by argument to maintain, their opinion in matters of religion, and that the same shall in no wise diminish, enlarge or affect their civil capacities.

Finally there stands his unequivocal statement on religious rights, as found in his letter to the Religious Society of Quakers, October, 1789:

The liberty enjoyed by the people of these States, of worshipping Almighty God agreeably to their consciences, is not only among the choicest of their *blessings,* but also of their *rights.* While men perform their social duties faithfully, they do all that society or the state can with propriety demand or expect; and remain responsible only to their Maker for the religion, or modes of faith, which they may prefer or profess.

Not only by words did George Washington express his approval of the principle of separation of church and state and all that is involved and implied by it, but he did his part to write it clear and large upon the fundamental documents of the state and the nation. Though the credit of authorship of the legal instruments by which religious liberty was achieved goes to such men as Mason, Madison, and Jefferson, Washington always labored sympathetically by their side. The study of the championship of religious liberty shows that Washington's name must always be linked with those of Madison, Hamilton, Jefferson, and Marshall.

The spirit which through the ages put obstacles in the way of religious liberty supported and justified itself by the contention succinctly phrased by St. Chrysostom, in the fifth century: "Nothing is more precious than a soul; the entire universe is not equal in value to it." From that starting point, as Luigi Luzzatti says in his *God in Free-*

dom, ardent faith develops into the mania of proselytizing, which

becomes irritated by resistance and is persuaded that the stubborn must be compelled, by every means, to acknowledge the one true God. And then all good instincts unite with the wicked impulses, first whispering councils of intolerance, which are hardly noticed, and then bursting forth impetuously, transforming angelic souls into frenzied demons. The passage from the phase of persuasion to that of persecution is easy, the purpose of earthly domination nearly always being hidden under the forms of religious proselytism.

Early history brings us largely the records of state religions which are accorded specific advantages and power, while all other forms of religious worship are decried and nearly always ruthlessly dealt with. Many of the saddest pages, the darkest and bloodiest, are those that deal with the haughty pontiffs of state religions and their efforts to stamp out other forms of the worship of God.

From the beginning, in fact, all nations had their state religions with the closest kind of connection between government and church, between priest and ruler. Yet in the earliest form of this union a sort of liberality was demonstrated toward those of another nation, and therefore of another faith. If only they paid due respect to the gods of their adopted country or of their temporary sojourn, as the case may be, they might continue to worship their own gods without molestation. In his *The Religious Teachers of Greece,* J. Adams says, "There was comparatively little persecution for religious beliefs in Greek antiquity." It was only when Rome became a world empire and the city of Rome a center of migrations, and a complex of diverse religions, that religious persecution became habitual. The Roman Twelve Tables laid down the law, *Nemo privatim habesset deos* (No one shall have private

7

gods) — apart and in addition, that is, to the public gods, the gods of the Roman pantheon. Rome became adept in persecution of religions, as none of the earlier nations did, probably because for the first time in history the Roman nation was confronted with two religions, Judaism and Christianity, whose adherents would not and could not worship the heathen gods in addition to the one God, and persistently refused to participate in Roman religious ceremonies.

Furthermore, the missionary zeal of the Jews and Christians also helps to explain the hostility of the Roman state religion to them. When political considerations made persecution unnecessary in Palestine and the missionary activities of the Jews flagged, Roman persecution of the Jew became insignificant. But Christianity invaded Rome and remained there as a missionary religion. Hence not only was it given the status of *religio nova et illicita,* a new and unlawful form of worship, but because it refused the ceremonies which the state religion required, and reviled its gods, its adherents were charged with atheism and treason. *Christianos ad leonem!* became the cry, and Nero burned Christians as torches to illumine his al fresco theatricals. In Trajan's time, about 112 A.D., Pliny the Younger had no doubt at all that the religion of the Christians marked them as worthy of death, quite apart from the crimes with which the Christians were charged who were brought before him while he was governor of Bithynia. At the beginning of the fourth century Diocletian ordered all churches to be destroyed, the Scriptures to be burned, the clergy to be imprisoned, and Christian officials to lose all civil rights. These edicts were followed by the great massacre at Eumenia and by wholesale burnings mentioned by Lactantius and Eusebius.

When Constantine placed the Christian religion in the favored position, it became the heir to this pagan Roman

8

conception of a state church, and, sad to say, bettered the instruction in persecution it had received from the older state religion. The Roman Empire was usually tolerant of local religions, especially if even perfunctory recognition was accorded the Roman pantheon along with the native gods, and frequently overlooked entire neglect of the Roman religious ceremonies if political issues were not involved. But the church, once in power in Rome, made no exceptions and had no leniency for what it chose to call atheism or heresy. It announced that heretics are more mischievous than criminals and that to rid the earth of them is just, beneficent, and necessary work. The virtues of heretics, such as they are, are no defense, claimed the philosophy of the church. *Splendida vitia*, the Church Fathers characterized them. Religion, to the church, was a fixed and definite quantity incapable of variation; it was a *depositum*, which must be defended by the civil sword if that could be enlisted in the service of the church. "Quae pejor mors animae quam libertas erroris?" (What is worse, death of the soul or liberty to err?), asked Constantine.

And so from Constantine to Philip II, from St. Augustine to Torquemada, the cruel consequences of this point of view held by the state church followed inevitably. Augustine, though most emphatic in asserting the inwardness of religion, paradoxically did more than anyone else to fasten the fetters of an ecclesiastical and dogmatic system upon mankind. He defended the church laws and procedures against heretics by comparing such laws to the restraint imposed upon lunatics or persons suffering under delirium, who would otherwise destroy themselves and others. So we have in the Code of Justinian (529 A.D.) a collection of all previous enactments against heretics, schismatics, pagans, and Jews, to which the church from time to time added others no less cruel and intolerant. For these decisions of the church concerning heresy, Isadore of Seville (636 A.D.) demands of the ruler every respect and enforcement by the secular power of the state.

Out of such outlooks and procedures the Inquisition, first an episcopal and later a papal tribunal, naturally arose. It sent to the flames of the auto-da-fé Albigenses, Waldenses, Spiritual Franciscans, and Jews. Not only were thousands upon thousands of these heretics burned, but Jews, Moors, Moriscos, and Christianized Moors who had relapsed were banished to the number of about three million in the course of a few centuries, while their property was confiscated. And in addition to this lurid record of religious intolerance, we discover the same forces of bigotry at work in the massacre of St. Bartholomew, in the Thirty Years War, in the persecution of the Brownists and Levellers in England, and so on down to the religious persecutions and pogroms in Russia during the period when Czar and Orthodox Greek Church were banded together to destroy heresies.

Throughout the entire history of religious persecution, however, we find many voices raised to plead for a far more liberal point of view, which sometimes even finds expression in the law. Most of these men spoke not for the separation of church and state, i.e., for complete religious liberty, but for toleration. In Rome three edicts of toleration were promulgated in the fourth century by Constantine and Licinius, and later by Emperor Maximin. The early Church Fathers advocated toleration. Lactantius maintained the inherent wickedness of persecution for religion. Toleration was the hallmark of the Renaissance. Sir Thomas More admitted its abstract excellence, and in his *Utopia* suggested, perhaps for the first time, the separation of church and state. Montaigne favored it. Erasmus labored incessantly for it. Yet with the exception of Zwingli, Socinus, and a few others, the leaders of the Reformation were not advocates of toleration.

Among the less important sects of the Reformation in the sixteenth century, the Anabaptists clearly enunciated the principle of the separation of church and state. They were followed by Robert Brown, leader of a group of Separatists who were known as Brownists, who stated the doctrine of separation in 1580. The seventeenth century saw the rise in England of the Separatists, a group of several sects, all of whom believed in separation from the established Church of England and also in separation of church and state. They were looked upon as infidels and heretics, and were tortured, imprisoned, and banished. But each sect of the Separatists was very certain that its dogmas were true and all the others false, and so amongst them there was much narrowness and bigotry and hatred. So the next forward step was taken by the Levellers, as they were called. John Lilburn, their leader, enunciated clearly and in no ambiguous terms the doctrine of freedom of conscience and of worship. His followers stood for the liberty of the individual as against the aggressions of government. They were the allies of Cromwell until his actions when he was in power demonstrated that he too could be narrow. Many of Lilburn's ideas and those of his group were promulgated by John Locke about 1690 and were later written into the American Constitution.

The voyagers who sailed westward in the *Mayflower* were largely Separatists and Levellers. John Robinson, a large-minded man of liberal views, drew up the covenant of the Pilgrim Fathers, the first instrument of which conferred equal civil and religious rights on every member of the commonwealth of New England which they founded. The charter of Charles I, founding the colony

11

of Maryland, granted toleration to Roman Catholics as well as Protestants.

It was about this time that John Milton was pleading eloquently in his *Areopagitica* not only for the freedom of the press, but also for religious toleration, curiously excepting Roman Catholics. In 1689 John Locke wrote the first of his four "Letters Concerning Toleration," basing his argument on the statement that the rightful sphere of the state is wholly confined to externals and does not extend to religion, which is internal. Here again we find surprisingly that while he advocates toleration for all Protestant sects and for Jews he does not extend it to Roman Catholics and atheists. Then Bayle in his *Dictionnaire* established the intellectual basis of toleration, holding it to be immoral to compel men to profess a religion they do not believe, and also irrational because it discourages the discovery of truth. So Montesquieu in *De L'esprit des Lois* (1748) exposes the futility of coercion in matters of religion, while Rousseau in his *Contrat Social* affirms the complete liberty of individual belief. But it was Voltaire above all who by his scathing sarcasm did more than any other man in France during the eighteenth century to put an end to religious persecution and to secure tolerance. Back of all these writings was a philosophy, developed largely in the eighteenth century, which tended powerfully toward the separation of church and state and toward complete religious liberty.

The American colonies fell heir to this double heritage from England and from France. The earliest champion in the colonies of religious liberty or "soul freedom," as he called it, was Roger Williams. He came to America on February 5, 1631, to escape the Laudian persecution. He was on terms of intimacy with Oliver Cromwell and was a friend of Milton. As Oscar S. Straus says in his book on *Origin of the Republican Form of Government*, to him

12

rightly belongs the immortal fame of having been the first person in modern times to assert and maintain in its fullest plenitude the absolute right of every man to enjoy "a full liberty in religious concernments" and to found a state having this doctrine as the keystone of its organic laws. Before Locke advocated the principle of toleration, before Milton wrote his *Eiconoclastes*, Roger Williams, the first pure type of the American freeman, proclaimed the laws of civil and religious liberty, that "the people were the origin of all free power in government"; that God has given to men no power over conscience, nor can men grant this power to each other; that the regulation of the conscience is not one of the purposes for which men combine in civil society.

Even the Puritans of Massachusetts colony, who "scrupled conformity" to several ceremonies of the established Church of England and who later fled to the Western Hemisphere from the persecutions of Laud, the Archbishop of Canterbury, could not abide such heresies. So Roger Williams and five companions founded the town of Providence, which he "desired . . . might be for shelter of persons distressed for conscience." This community of Providence enlarged into the colony of Rhode Island. All comers to the colony were required to subscribe to the following covenant or constitution:

We whose names are hereunder written, being desirous to inhabit the town of Providence, do promise to submit ourselves in active and passive obedience to all such orders or agreements as shall be made for public good of the body, in an orderly way, by the major consent of the present inhabitants . . . only in civil things.

This simple instrument is the earliest constitution of government whereof we have any record which not only tolerated all religions, but recognized as a right absolute liberty of conscience. In 1663, the colony of Rhode Island received a charter from Charles II containing this most important provision:

No person within the said colony at any time hereafter shall be in any wise molested, punished, disquieted or called in question for any differences in opinion, in matters of religion, who does not actually disturb the civil peace of our said colony; but that all and every person and persons may from time to time, and at all times hereafter, freely and fully, have and enjoy his own and their judgments and consciences, in matters of religious concernments.

As to priority of legal enactments respecting religious liberty, it may be noted that the law of Maryland was enacted in 1649, while in Rhode Island the first General Assembly in 1647 adopted a code of laws concluding with the words, "All men may walk as their consciences persuade them, everyone in the name of God." It may further be noted in comparing the liberality of Lord Baltimore, proprietor of the colony of Maryland, with that of Roger Williams, that whereas the charter of Lord Baltimore was fully a century ahead of its time, it evidently did not rise to the standard of Rhode Island, in that it extended religious freedom only to Christians.

The charter of the colony of Virginia, founded at Jamestown in 1607, enjoined the establishment of religion according to the doctrine and usages of the Church of England. In each parish all the inhabitants were taxed alike for the support of the churches of the established order. Several acts of the Virginia Assembly, of 1659, 1662, and 1693, made it a penal offense in parents to refuse to have their children baptized. But in half a century a complete change was effected. After the signing of the Declaration of Independence the Presbyterians of Hanover, Virginia, addressed the Virginia House of assembly in a memorial recommending, in a spirit of fairness and equal justice to all, a separation of church and state, leaving the support of the gospel to the voluntary efforts of its votaries. "In this enlightened age," the memorial states, "and in a land where all of every denomination are united in the most strenuous efforts to be free, we hope and expect that our representatives will cheerfully concur in removing every species of religious as well as civil bondage. Certain it is, that every argument for civil liberty gains additional strength when applied to liberty in the concerns of religion."

On June 12, 1776, the Virginia Constitutional Convention adopted a bill of rights amongst which was specifically mentioned the right to religious liberty. It must be be noted that the original draft of the bill of rights by George Mason went only part of the way, for no Anglo-Saxon tradition made religious liberty an inherent right of a free people, and accordingly the resolution drafted by Mason stated that "all men should enjoy the fullest toleration in the exercise of religion according to the dictates of conscience." James Madison, who was a member of that convention, pointed out that freedom of thought and conscience must not be confused with toleration and that the resolution did not go to the root of the matter. For the free exercise of religion according to the dictates of conscience is something which every man may demand as a right, not something for which he must ask as a privilege. To grant to the state the power of tolerating is implicitly to grant it that of prohibiting, whereas Madison would deny to it any jurisdiction whatever in the matter of religion. The substitute resolution offered by Madison protected that right in the fullest manner:

That religion, or the duty we owe our Creator, and the manner of discharging it, being under the direction of the reason and conviction only, not of violence or compulsion, all men are equally entitled to the full and free exercise of it, according to the dictates of conscience, and therefore no man or class of men ought on account of religion be invested with peculiar emoluments or privileges, nor subjected to any penalties or disabilities, unless under color of religion the preservation of equal liberty and the existence of the state be manifestly endangered.

The convention agreed that for the word "toleration" should be substituted the doctrine of right of free exercise of religion; but as a body they were unwilling to adopt prohibition of peculiar emoluments or privileges to the adherents of a particular church. In the final form the clause adopted was:

That religion, or the duty we owe to our Creator, and the manner of discharging it, can be directed only by reason and conviction, not by force or violence and therefore all men are equally entitled to the free exercise of religion according to the dictates of conscience, and that it is the mutual duty of all to practice Christian forbearance, love and charity toward each other.

Even with this constitution, Virginia was not entirely purged of union of church and state. Under Jefferson's lead during the Revolution, however, obnoxious law after law was repealed, and annual proposed assessments for the maintenance of the established church failed of passage. In connection with these latter attempts Jefferson drafted the famous bill of 1779, whose enactment Madison secured in 1785 and which was entitled "Act for Establishing Religious Freedom." Its three sections contain the finest utterances on religious freedom to be found in any legal document. Its second section reads:

We, the General Assembly of Virginia, do enact that no man shall be compelled to frequent or support any religious worship, place or ministry whatsoever, nor shall be enforced,

16

restrained, molested, or otherwise burdened in his body or goods, nor shall otherwise suffer on account of his religious opinions or belief; but that all men shall be free to possess, and by argument to maintain, their opinion in matters of religion, and that the same shall in no wise diminish, enlarge, or affect their civil capacities.

The third section states that while this Assembly recognizes that it has no power to restrain acts of succeeding Assemblies, and therefore cannot declare this act to be irrevocable, yet "we are free to declare that the rights hereby asserted are of the nature of natural rights of mankind, and that if any act shall be hereafter passed to repeal the present or to narrow its operation, such act will be an infringement of natural right." So proud was Jefferson of his services in this cause that in the epitaph which he prepared to be placed on his tombstone he linked with the words "Author of the Declaration of Independence" the further words "of the Statute of Virginia for Religious Liberty." That George Washington favored the point of view expressed by this act may be noted by his letter of October 3, 1775, when Virginia was struggling over the question of religious assessments, in which he says that "no man's sentiments are more opposed to any kind of restraint upon religious principles than mine are."

Doubtless the early efforts to promote religious liberty in Virginia had their direct influence in the other colonies. In November, 1776, measures to the same effect were adopted by the legislature of Maryland, and the union of church and state was in like manner dissolved by the legislatures in New York, South Carolina, and the other colonies in which the Protestant Episcopal church was predominant. Connecticut and Massachusetts were the last to yield to the advancing tide of religious liberty. It was not until 1816 that the connection was dissolved in

17

Connecticut, and not until 1833 that this happened in Massachusetts.

The Pennsylvania constitution, adopted September 28, 1776, contains the provision:

That all men have a natural and inalienable right to worship God according to the dictates of their own consciences and understanding, and that no man ought or of right can be compelled to attend any religious worship or erect and support any place of worship or maintain any ministry contrary to and against his own free will and consent; nor can any man who acknowledges the being of a God be justly deprived of any civil right as a citizen on account of his religious sentiments or peculiar mode of religious worship, and that no authority can or ought to be vested in or assumed by any power that shall in any case interfere with or in any manner control the right of conscience in the free exercise of religious worship.

This provision, while going farther in some respects than the Virginia statement, is weakened by the fact that it does not admit the right of a citizen to deny conscientiously "the existence of a God," and further vitiated by a religious test for office in the following declaration to which officers must subscribe: "I do believe in one God, the creator and governor of the Universe, the rewarder of the good and the punisher of the wicked, and I do acknowledge the scriptures of the Old and New Testament to be given by divine inspiration." Franklin, who presided at this convention, disapproved of this test, but accepted it upon the practical consideration that it might prevent others in the future from imposing a more drastic one.

In the constitutional convention held in New York in 1777, the original draft of the provision for religious freedom, prepared in a committee of which John Jay, William Duer, Gouverneur Morris, Robert Livingston, and William

Yates were members, contained a phrase providing that "free toleration be forever allowed." Before adoption by the convention it was changed, as in Virginia, to "free exercise and enjoyment of religious profession and worship." Further, this free exercise of religious worship was originally offered "to all denominations of Christians, without preference or distinction, and to all Jews, Turks and Infidels," subject to limitation where the legislature might determine a particular doctrine to be "incompatible with and repugnant to the peace, safety and welfare of civil society in general and this state in particular." This provision was amended in the committee itself in the most liberal spirit, though the debates evinced a certain doubt as to the wisdom of giving this free exercise of religious worship to the Roman Catholic church. John Jay proposed an amendment to the effect that to the general principle of religious freedom an exception should be inserted affecting the holding of land and participation in civil rights by Catholics until they appeared before the supreme court of the state and swore that no pope, priest, or foreign authority on earth had power to absolve the subjects of the state from their allegiance to it. But the convention under the leadership of Gouverneur Morris and Chancellor Livingston not only defeated the amendment by a vote of nineteen to ten, but also finally adopted a resolution couched in ringing words:

Whereas we are required by the benevolent principles of rational liberty, not only to expel civil tyranny, but also to guard against spiritual oppression and intolerance wherewith the bigotry and ambition of weak and wicked priests have scourged mankind, this convention does further in the name and by the authority of the good people of this state ordain, determine and declare that the free exercise and enjoyment of religious profession and worship without discrimination or preference shall, hereafter, be allowed within this state to all

19

mankind. Provided that the liberty of conscience hereby granted shall not be so construed as to excuse acts of licentiousness.

When the Federal Constitutional Convention was called in 1787, much of the work of disestablishment had been accomplished, though in many states complete religious liberty was still unattained. As no two of the American colonies were precisely alike in religious complexion, it was impossible, as Judge Joseph Story points out, that there should not arise perpetual strife and jealousy if the national government were left free to create a religious establishment. But the denial of this power alone would have been an imperfect security, if it had not been followed up by an affirmative declaration of the right of the free exercise of religion and a prohibition of all religious tests.

The question of religious liberty was first broached in the Federal Constitutional Convention by Charles Pinckney of South Carolina, who, on May 29, 1787, in his proposed draft of the Constitution embodied a clause reading, "The legislature of the United States shall pass no law on the subject of religion." On August 20, 1787, he suggested an amendment to the effect that "no religious test or qualification shall ever be annexed to any office under the United States." When early in June, 1787, the provision for an oath for public officers to support the Constitution came up in the debates, and the words "or affirmation" were added after "oath," so as to meet the religious scruples of Quakers, Pinckney moved to add to this article the words, "but no religious test shall ever be required as a qualification to any office or public trust under the authority of the United States." This motion was unanimously adopted. No effort was made to enact a further religious liberty clause, because the convention decided

20

that no bill of rights in which such a clause would most appropriately appear was necessary, as they held the theory that the federal government would have only such rights as were expressly granted to it. But the unanimous vote on the motion of Charles Pinckney as to a religious test shows clearly the attitude of the convention on the question.

Again, when on the eighteenth of August, 1787, Charles Pinckney suggested that Congress should be authorized to establish a university, the motion was recast upon the suggestion of Madison to read, "To establish a university, in which no reference or distinction should be allowed on account of religion." The resolution was defeated, but only on the ground that it was unnecessary since "the exclusive power of the Seat of Government will reach the object." The question of religious liberty was once more brought up somewhat informally when Alexander Hamilton suggested to the convention in his proposed constitution a comprehensive religious liberty provision reading, "Nor shall any religious sect or religious denomination or religious test for any office or place be ever established by law." Though it was not adopted, it showed that he too, like his rival Jefferson, was an ardent advocate of religious liberty.

When the drafted Constitution was published, considerable objection arose to the absence of a bill of rights, especially one assuring religious liberty. Thomas Jefferson was the main leader in voicing such objection. Writing from Paris to Madison on December 20, 1787, he said, "I will now add what I do not like; first, the omission of a bill of rights, providing clearly and without the aid of sophisms, for freedom of religion, freedom of the press, etc." Much of the reluctance of the states to adopt the Constitution came from the absence of a bill of rights, and Elliott's *Debates* shows that in the conventions of almost every state some objection was expressed that there was no restriction upon the federal government with respect to legislation regarding religion. In Massachusetts, Virginia, and North Carolina the conventions for ratification spent much time on the religious liberty provisions and gave them much attention in their debates. In the Virginia convention the absence of a prohibition of federal impairment of religious liberty was one of the chief arguments of those who opposed ratification, particularly Patrick Henry. An amendment to the Constitution proposed by a group of the members, among whom were Patrick Henry, Governor Randolph, George Mason, Madison, Monroe, Tyler, and John Marshall, based on the Virginia Bill of Rights but improving it materially, read:

That religion, or the duty we owe to our Creator, and the manner of discharging it can be directed only by reason and conviction, not by force or violence; and therefore all men have an equal, natural and inalienable right to the free exercise of religion, according to the dictates of conscience, and that no particular religious sect or society ought to be favored or established by law, in preference to others.

After the first Congress under the Constitution was elected, Washington, John Adams, Hamilton, and Jefferson threw their influence in favor of the adoption of a religious liberty bill of rights clause, and the task of securing its adoption was assumed by James Madison, unquestionably the most distinguished and influential member of that Congress. On June 8, 1789, Madison offered a series of proposed constitutional amendments including one concerning religious liberty which read as follows:

The civil rights of none shall be abridged on account of religious belief or worship, nor shall any national religion be established, nor shall the full and equal rights of conscience be in any manner or on any pretext infringed.... No state shall violate the equal rights of conscience or the freedom of the press, or the trial by jury in criminal cases.

The final form of the religious liberty clause as it appeared as the first amendment to the Constitution is: "Congress shall make no law respecting an establishment of religion or prohibiting the free exercise thereof."

It has been claimed by many students of this period (among them being Max J. Kohler, to whose fine summary of the religious liberty struggle in the United States entitled *The Fathers of the Republic and Constitutional Establishment of Religious Liberty* the writer is deeply indebted) that without the support of George Washington the first amendment would not have been approved by Congress. His espousal of the cause of absolute religious liberty in the Virginia struggle and his attitude of opposition to religious tests in the Federal Constitutional Convention over which he presided were climaxed by his efforts for the passage of the first amendment.

This first amendment was, as Luigi Luzzatti terms it in his great work, *God in Freedom,* the habeas corpus of the soul. It recognized free religions in a sovereign state. It gave practical effect to Paine's words: "Toleration is not the opposite to intoleration, but the counterfeit of it. Both are despotisms. The one assumes the right of withholding liberty of conscience, and the other of granting it." A century later, in an official state paper on the Keily case, Secretary of State Thomas F. Bayard said with the express approval of President Grover Cleveland:

Religious liberty is the chief cornerstone of the American system of government, and provisions for its security are embedded in the written charter and interwoven in the moral fabric of its laws. Anything that tends to invade a right so essential and sacred must be carefully guarded against, and I am satisfied that my countrymen, ever mindful of the suffer-

ing and sacrifices necessary to obtain it, will never consent to
its impairment for any reason or under any pretext whatsoever.

The divorce between church and state so enthusiasti-
cally ordered by the Constitutional Fathers, the First
Congress, and the great body of the nation represented
by them, was only gradually consummated by each one
of the states of the union as they annulled many of their
old laws based upon a different philosophy of government. B. H. Hartogensis, a member of the Baltimore bar
and a diligent student of the nullifications of the religious
liberty amendments, has drawn up, in the *Yale Law
Journal* of March, 1930, a list of indictments in the matter
of the Denial of Equal Rights to Religious Minorities and
Non-believers of the United States. He not only shows
how some of the states were rather slow in making their
state laws agree in spirit and procedure with the first and
sixth amendments to the Federal Constitution, but points
out decisions of legal authorities and high court judges
which do not rise to the high demand of those amendments. He shows that until 1877 New Hampshire required
that its state senators and representatives should be of
the Protestant religion. Like restrictive words were formerly used in the constitutions of Delaware, South Carolina, Massachusetts, Connecticut, and Vermont.

The constitution of Arkansas prescribes that "No person
who denies the being of a God shall hold any office in
the civil departments of the State or be competent to
testify as a witness in any court." Tennessee's constitution
has almost the same words, except as to competency of
witnesses. In North Carolina, the constitution of 1868
ordered that "all persons who shall deny the being of
God are disqualified from office." Under Pennsylvania's
present constitution "no person who acknowledges the
being of God or a future state of rewards and punish-

ments shall on account of his religious opinions be so disqualified," which suggests that those who do not so believe may be disqualified. In Maryland the Code of Public General Laws (1924) prescribes for the oath of office a declaration of belief in the Christian religion, though the present constitution of the state prescribes that there shall be no test "other than a declaration of belief in the existence of God" (Constitution of Maryland [1867], Declaration of Rights, article 37).

Besides these relics of the union of church and state we note that from time to time groups of American citizens have attempted to nullify not only the constitutional guarantees but the very spirit of the founders of the Republic by seeking to introduce Bible reading in the public schools, frequently giving that ceremony the flavor of a religious service by the introduction of hymns of a sectarian nature. Other groups of our citizens have from time to time proposed that a recognition of Christianity be inserted into the fundamental document of our country on the ground that this is a Christian nation. A straightforward answer was given these proponents in a decision rendered on March 12, 1932, by Judge Eugene O'Dunne of the Superior Court of Baltimore City. The new Baltimore Sunday ordinance had been attacked in the courts on the ground that it "is an assault on the Christian religion which is part of the common law of the state of Maryland, and upon which its policy is founded." After hearing all the evidence throughout one week, Judge O'Dunne handed down his decision, in which we read:

... my decision is, as far as the first proposition is concerned, that Christianity is not part of the common law of Maryland as a legal proposition; that it is not part of the common law of England; and that it is not the function of any Court in this country, where church and state are separated, to undertake to infuse religious principles that an individual personally may believe in, and try to use the medium of law as a vehicle to further Christianity, or to further his conception of Christianity, and to get them incorporated in the body politic. That is no function of government. We are not a Christian nation in the legal sense at all.

Because of the many relics in our state constitutions of provisions contrary to the principle of the separation of church and state, the many attempts to nullify the articles on religious liberty in our Federal Constitution, and the sinister spirit that from time to time manifests itself in seeking to deny American citizenship to all but American-born and Protestants, it is well to rehearse the inspiring story whose culmination is found in that great document, our Constitution, in the various steps of whose formulation George Washington took a lively interest and often a decisive part. One may hope that a renewed allegiance to the spirit of that document, especially as manifested in the efforts of its authors to found a government free from tyranny, civil and religious, will spring from our recurrence to the fundamental principles it sets forth.

THE RELATION OF THE LIFE AND PHILOSOPHY
OF SPINOZA TO JUDAISM

I T IS SURELY always appropriate to present a serious
study of Spinoza, and certainly no apology need
preface such a presentation at any time; for if it
is true, as a nineteenth-century philosopher said, that
"to be a Hegelian one must first be a Spinozist," it is
equally true that to know the basis of all modern philosophy you must be familiar with the *Ethics,* with the *Short
Treatise,* with the *Tractatus Theologico-Politicus,* and with
the *Treatise on the Improvement of the Understanding.*
And if this is so at all times, how much more on the 250th
anniversary of the death of the great lens grinder of
Amsterdam, and before a group of students both of
Judaism and of philosophy.

The title of this paper delimits the treatment very
clearly. It suggests that it is not the intention of this
discussion to present a thoroughgoing study of either the
life or the philosophy of Spinoza. Nor will it enter deeply
into the question quite interestingly discussed in the
Menorah Journal of February, 1927, whether Spinozism
is in harmony with Jewish tradition. It will seek to present
certain important relations which both Spinoza's life and
his philosophy have with Judaism. It will try to determine
how far we Jews can claim that "this greatest modern philosopher" based his search for truth upon his
Jewish experiences and his Jewish studies and Jewish
forebears. It is in brief an effort to place Baruch Spinoza
where he surely belongs and where we could be proud to

Paper read before the Kallah of Texas Rabbis, 1932.

see him, near the head of the long line of notable Jewish thinkers of the ages — instead of being, as he has been up to recent date, cast out from that high company, with Maimonides the Aristotelian the leader, while out in limbo was Spinoza and Spinozism standing before the heresy of Pantheism, the heresy which identifies God with corporeal being and thus approaches material atheism. Obviously such a verdict of the long ago must have been unjust, for surely if Spinozism were the horrible heresy painted by its opponents there would not now be the great pilgrimage to the author of the *Ethics*, and we would not be witnessing the spectacle of the unbeliever of the twentieth century being converted to a belief in God by the seventeenth-century Jew who was excommunicated from the synagogue for his monstrous opinions. In a word, this is a belated and humble effort to bring him again close to the bosom of the people that cast him out.

Let us view the important incidents of his life and note how close the elements thereof are to Judaism. Baruch Spinoza was born into a family of marranos, who had made their way from Portugal early in the seventeenth century and had settled in the more hospitable Netherlands in the city of Amsterdam. Both the grandfather, Abraham Espinoza, and the father, Michael Espinoza, held synagogal offices. So Baruch was brought up and taught as a Jewish child usually is. He studied Hebrew, the Bible in the original, was Bar Mitzvah and then continued the higher Jewish studies under Rabbi Saul de Morteira and Rabbi Manasseh ben Israel. At eighteen he refused to enter business, which was not to his taste, and he took up the art of polishing lenses, which many learned men of that generation had adopted. No doubt he did not openly offend the synagogue until after the death of his father in 1654, when Baruch was in his twenty-second year.

It is important in connection with the subject of this paper to note the character of Spinoza's education and to discover how completely he was being formed in the Jewish mold. The Amsterdam Jewish community had their own Jewish boys' school, which was founded in 1638, and which all Jewish boys attended as a matter of course. The general curriculum of this school is known from contemporary accounts. We also know the names and characters of some of its most important teachers in the time of Spinoza. There were seven classes in the school and the subjects taught in the various classes were like those being taught in the modern Talmud Torah. He went through all the classes and therefore had studied his Torah, Neviim and Kesuvim, Rashi's Commentary, Hebrew Grammar, portions of the Talmud and the later Hebrew Codes, Ibn Ezra, Maimonides and others according to the discretion and special interest of the teacher. We are explicitly informed that during the hours that the boys were at home they would receive private instruction in secular subjects, even in verse making. The school had a good lending library. Spinoza came under the powerful influence during his school years of Rabbi Saul Morteira and Rabbi Manasseh ben Israel. Saul Morteira was the chief Rabbi of Amsterdam. Born in Venice about 1596, he studied medicine under Montalto, the marrano court physician of Maria de Medici. Montalto died suddenly while accompanying Louis XIII to Tours, in 1616, and it was the desire of Montalto to be buried in a Jewish cemetery that brought Saul de Morteira to Amsterdam where the Jews had in 1614 acquired a cemetery at Ouwerkerk, not far from the city. While in Amsterdam Morteira accepted the call to the rabbinate of the older of the two synagogues there (the House of Jacob). Morteira had had a taste of court life, and was not altogether wanting in philosophical appreciation; but he was essentially medieval, strait-laced, prosy, and uninspiring. It is related that when Spinoza was but a fifteen-year-old lad Morteira marvelled at the boy's acumen. By an irony of fate he also presided over the rabbinical court which issued the ban against Spinoza in 1656.

In Manasseh ben Israel we have a different type of character altogether. He was born in 1604 and had a tragic infancy. His father, Joseph ben Israel, was one of a hundred and fifty Jews whom the inquisition in Lisbon was about to consign to the flames in 1605 when a million gold florins, eight hundred thousand ducats, and five hundred thousand crusados were paid to Philip III, and a hundred thousand crusados to the saintly ecclesiastics to reconcile them to sparing their victims the flames of hell on earth, even if it should entail their loss of heaven hereafter. After this terrible experience Joseph ben Israel naturally at the first opportunity fled with his wife and infant son, Manasseh, to Amsterdam where Manasseh lived nearly all his life. He succeeded his teacher Rabbi Uzziel as rabbi of the second Amsterdam Synagogue (Beth Sholom) in 1622 when he was barely eighteen years old; started a Hebrew printing press about 1627; was about to emigrate in 1640 to Brazil when he received an important appointment in the Amsterdam Jewish School where Spinoza must have come under his influence.

Manasseh was not a great thinker, but he was a great reader, and made up in breadth of outlook what he lacked in depth of insight. Like so many of his contemporary theologians, he was inclined toward mysticism. This very mysticism prompted him to schemes that appeared quixotic, and which brought about his untimely end, but which bore fruit nevertheless. What he conceived to be his mission in life is indicated in the Biblical verse with which he headed the dedication of his *Esperanza de*

Israel (Hope of Israel) in 1650. The book, it is interesting to observe, was dedicated to Spinoza's father and the other wardens of the Jewish school. At the head of the dedication is the first verse from Isaiah 61, "To preach good tidings unto the meek; he hath sent me to bind up the broken-hearted." In 1655 Manasseh came to England on a special mission to Oliver Cromwell for the readmission of the Jews into England. Two years later he returned to the Netherlands carrying with him the corpse of his eldest son. His great schemes seemed shattered. Poor, prematurely aged, and full of sorrows, he died in Middleburg in 1657.

Manasseh ben Israel was fluent, it is said, in ten languages, and we know he wrote books in Hebrew, Latin, Dutch, Spanish, and Portuguese. What is more likely than that he should use his influence with Spinoza's father so that Baruch might be taught Latin and other secular subjects? And what is more natural than that Manasseh, who encouraged and helped his Christian friend, a son of Gerhard Vossius, to study and translate Maimonides, should have been even more eager to urge his Jewish students to study their own Hispano-Jewish literature, of which they were justly proud? At the house of his rabbi, Spinoza would occasionally meet Christians who were interested in Judaism, or in the Jewish interpretation of the Old Testament. Here he may have met Rembrandt, who between 1640 and 1656 lived in the very heart of the Jewish quarter and was probably on friendly terms with the "Amsterdam Rabbi," as Manasseh was called. For Rembrandt etched a portrait of Manasseh in 1636, and illustrated one of his books (the *Piedra Gloriosa*, published in 1655). Moreover, in the Hermitage at St. Petersburg there is a Rembrandt painting of a rabbi aged and worn and believed to be Manasseh ben Israel.

Above all, the moral earnestness of Manasseh was conspicuous. He was an earnest disciple and an earnest master. He was an earnest and eloquent preacher and he probably passed on some of his master's moral earnestness to his pupil Spinoza. The latter must also have obtained from his teacher a goodly knowledge of the Kabbalistic literature which we will show influenced him deeply in the development of his philosophic system. Therefore, apart from the few non-Jews whom probably he met at Rabbi Manasseh ben Israel's house and apart from Francis van den Enden, an ex-Jesuit, ex-diplomat, ex-bookseller, doctor and classicist to whose school in Amsterdam Spinoza went to complete his secular studies, it is seen that his whole outlook and training and sources of influence were Jewish up to the year 1654, and up to the period that just preceded his excommunication.

Spinoza had an inborn passion for clear and consistent thinking. The great intellectual gifts with which fortune had unstintingly endowed him were of course abundantly exercised and sharpened in the prolonged study of the Talmud and codes, abounding as they do in subtle problems and subtler solutions. Their value as a mental discipline was undeniable. Moreover, quite apart from this sharpening of his reasoning powers the use of which carried him into antagonism with the synagogue, his other Hebrew studies provided him also with ample material and stimulus for the exercise of his critical acumen which again set him at odds with the Jewish religious authorities. The spirit of rationalism pervades the whole literature of the Jews of the Spanish period, and the masterpieces of that literature were the pride of the Jewish refugees from the Peninsula, indeed of all Jews. In the commentary of Abraham Ibn Ezra (1092-1167) Spinoza found many bold and suggestive hints. In the preface, Ibn Ezra states that he "will show no partiality in the exposition of the law," and although the promise seems bolder than the fulfilment, yet now and then one meets with "a word to the wise," which is just sufficient to direct attention to some inconsistency in the Scripture, to the post-Mosaic authorship of certain passages in the Pentateuch, or to the different authorship of the first and second parts of Isaiah. These hints, obscure as they may seem, justify Ibn Ezra's claim to be called the father of Higher Criticism of the Bible, and they certainly led to Spinoza's subsequent important contributions to this kind of Bible criticism.

In the *More Nebuchim* of Maimonides (1135-1204) his attention was drawn to certain crudities and inconsistencies in Biblical theology, which Maimonides indeed tried to explain away or to reconcile with the requirements of reason — though apparently, in the judgment of Spinoza, with little success. And Maimonides' treatment of the institution of sacrifices as merely a temporary concession or device to wean away Israel from idolatry could not but suggest to Spinoza that other religious customs, too, were only temporary in character and validity. In the writings of Gersonides (1288-1344) he saw rationalism encroaching on miracles and on prophecy, so as to explain away their supposed supernatural character. Maimonides had already boldly asserted that any passage of the Bible that appeared to conflict with reason must be so interpreted as to be in harmony with it. This method of "interpreting" Scripture into conformity with reason still seemed to save the priority of the Bible over reason — though only in appearance. Gersonides went farther than that. Frankly admitting the possibiilty of a real conflict between reason and revelation, he openly declared that the Bible "cannot prevent us from holding that to be true which our reason prompts us to believe."

Furthermore, the Jews were affected, like the rest of the thinking world, by the Renaissance with its tendency toward free thought. Thus Joseph Delmedigo arrived in Amsterdam in 1628 fresh from his studies in the University of Padua. He was well versed in philosophy, medicine, physics, and mathematics, as well as in Hebrew literature, and he also had studied astronomy under Galileo. He seems to have stayed several years in Amsterdam, where Manasseh ben Israel published a selection of his works. He was a remarkable product of that age of conflict between the old and the new. Unsettled by the new spirit of the age, yet faithful to the old, his mind inclined now toward skepticism and again toward mysticism, and his nomad life was a typical expression of a restless, vacillating mind seeking in vain to gain its equilibrium.

To judge from contemporary complaints, Amsterdam Jewry had not a few such religious malcontents, and the leaders had to cope with the trouble as best they could. In 1623 Samuel da Silva, a Jewish physician at Amsterdam, was called upon to write a defense of the immortality of the soul and the inspiration of the Bible against the skeptical views aired by Uriel Acosta. In 1632 Manasseh ben Israel published the first part of the *Conciliator*, wherein he sought to reconcile the apparent inconsistencies of the Scripture, a textbook needed by the many marranos who were constantly coming to the Netherlands, surrendering Catholicism and adopting Judaism and turning to the Bible there to discover many perplexing contradictions.

Thus this clear thinker coming under these influences soon found himself in antagonism with official Judaism. That it brought on the drastic consequences of an excommunication was the result of a number of special circumstances. The Jewish community in the Netherlands was largely composed of marrano Jews who had slipped out of Portugal and Spain after over a century of overt Cathol-

icism in many cases. These returning Jews, many of them
with an almost complete Christian theological background, had to be re-educated into Judaism. It was hardly
a normal Jewish community; heterodoxy of any sort could
not be tolerated there as easily as in other Jewish groups.
Then, toleration was not anywhere in the atmosphere
about them. The decree of toleration embodied in the
Treaty of Utrecht did not secure much of real toleration.
Non-Calvinist Christians were allowed to live in the
Netherlands without suffering in person or property on
account of nonconformity. For those days even that was
a great deal; but the right of public worship was quite
another matter. And if the Union of Utrecht did not
secure real toleration for all Christian sects, much less
did it guarantee anything to the Jews, who had not been
contemplated in it at all, who had not even been formally admitted into the Netherlands, but whose presence
had been more or less connived at. Even in 1619, when
the Jewish question was definitely raised in the Netherlands, it was decided to allow each city to please itself
whether it would permit the Jews to live there or not.
Their position was precarious indeed. They had to take
care not to give offense to the religious susceptibilities of
their neighbors. Their troubles in this direction com-
menced soon enough.

About the year 1618 there arrived in Amsterdam a marrano refugee from Portugal whose name was Gabriel
Acosta. Both he and his father had held office in the
Catholic church, but seized by sudden longing to return
to the religion of his ancestors, Gabriel fled to Amsterdam,
where he embraced Judaism and changed his name from
Gabriel to Uriel. His ideas about Judaism had been
derived chiefly from reading the Old Testament, and his
contact with rabbinic Judaism somewhat disappointed
him. He thereupon began to speak disrespectfully and

contemptuously of the Jews as Pharisees, and aired his views freely against the belief in immortality of the soul and the inspiration of the Bible. These views were of course as much opposed to Christianity as to Judaism. The Jewish physician, Da Silva, tried to controvert them in a book published in 1623. Acosta replied in 1624, with a treatise which was very confused and which, while accusing Da Silva of slander against the author, actually reiterated those heresies.

Partly from fear that an outcry might be raised against the Jews as promulgators of heresy, the Jewish authorities excommunicated Uriel Acosta, and as a kind of official repudiation of all responsibility for him, they communicated the facts to the civil authorities, who thereupon imprisoned and fined him and ordered his book to be burned. Shunned by Jews and Christians alike, Acosta found his existence very lonely and intolerable; and in 1633 he made up his mind, as he said, "to become an ape among apes," and made his peace with the synagogue. But he soon got quite reckless again and was excommunicated a second time. Again he grew weary of isolation, and once more approached the authorities of the synagogue for the removal of the ban. Determined not to be duped again, yet reluctant to repel him absolutely, they imposed hard conditions on him. He submitted to them — he recanted his sins publicly in the synagogue, received thirty-nine lashes, and lay prostrate on the threshold of the synagogue while the congregation stepped over him as they passed out. It was a cruel degradation, and so heavily did his humiliation weigh on his mind that he committed suicide soon after. This happened in 1640. Spinoza may have witnessed the terrible scene and must have remembered the scandal.

If the Jewish community of Amsterdam felt it necessary to repudiate in such a drastic manner their responsibility for Uriel Acosta's heresies, so as to avoid giving offense to their Christian neighbors, there was every reason why they should feel even greater discomfort on account of Spinoza's heresies in 1656. It was a critical period in the annals of Jewish history. During the Cossack and Muscovite invasion of Poland (1654-1656) entire Jewish communities were massacred by the invaders; nor did the Poles behave much better toward the Jews during the war. Naturally whosoever could tried to escape from the scene of the slaughter. There was consequently a considerable influx of Polish Jews into Amsterdam.

The Jewish community in Amsterdam did not gain in security, we may be sure, through the influx of these destitute refugees. Then more than ever it was necessary to be circumspect to avoid giving offense to the people of the land, especially on that most delicate point, religion. They did not want another scandal. One Acosta affair was enough. So, after many fruitless attempts to make him silent, they tried to bribe Spinoza, promising him a considerable annuity if he would only keep quiet and show some outward conformity to his religion. Of course they knew that outward conformity, because of a price, would not stamp out heresy; rather would it make it attractive by rendering it profitable. The real motive was fear of jeopardizing the position of the Jewish community, though perhaps they did not realize it so explicitly.

If they had urged these points on Spinoza he would undoubtedly have appreciated the need for caution and silence. But they evidently did not understand him and misconceived his character entirely, and the attempt to gag him by a bribe was just the way best calculated to defeat their end. The only person who might have understood him was Manasseh ben Israel, but he was in England on a mission to Cromwell. So threats were next tried; but the threat of excommunication had no effect. They

had reached the end of their tether and some time in
June 1656 he was summoned before the court of rabbis.
Witnesses gave evidences of his heresies, namely that the
Bible was not inspired, that there are no angels, and that
the soul is not immortal. He was excommunicated for a
period of thirty days in the hope that he might relent.
But he did not, and on July 27, 1656, the final ban was
pronounced upon him publicly in the synagogue of Amsterdam. The three forms of ban known to the Jews and
employed by them, at all times most sparingly, were the
N'fizah, the *Niddui,* a ban for seven or thirty days on
account of monetary matters, and lastly the most drastic,
the *Herem.* It was the last that was pronounced by the
synagogue officials upon Spinoza, and was read out in
public according to the traditional formula. And in judging the officials let us remember that the ban against
Spinoza was the due paid to Caesar, rather than to the
God of Israel. Heresies were not so run down as a custom-
ary thing amongst the Jews. Even Elisha ben Abuya, the
Faust of the Talmud, was not persecuted by the Jews;
no *Herem* was pronounced upon him, in spite of his
heresies.

Though he willingly submitted to the physical separation from his people from this time on, as imposed upon
him by his excommunication, the activities of Spinoza's
mind were ever close to Jewish ethics, Jewish philosophy.
In his spiritual outlook he never left the Jewish people.
Though he fell afoul of the Jewish officials of the synagogue by his arguments against the divine inspiration of
the Torah, by his insistence that its contents show no
outflowing of divine wisdom, but rather the work of
fallible human authors, though he raised the banner of
historical criticism and even stormed the Talmud, yet
much of his Bible criticism originated with Ibn Ezra,
Gersonides, Rashi, Kimchi, Azariah de Rossi, and Crescas.

38

It can well be shown that his philosophy is influenced tremendously in his *Tractatus Theologico-Politicus* by Maimonides; his theory of God as the One substance and
thought of the Universe is based largely on Jewish Kabbala of the *Zohar;* and his *Ethics* is founded in no incon-
siderable degree on the *Or Adonoi* of Crescas.

The point that Spinoza knew and made use of the
Bible criticism of early medieval Jewish scholars like Ibn
Ezra and Crescas is too well known to labor much upon
it. However, that the philosophy and ethics of Spinoza
were developed with a large and wide dependence on
the works and even the words of Maimuni, the *Zohar,*
and Crescas may need more than mere mention. Without
Maimonides whole chapters of the *Tractatus* could hardly
have been possible. Of course Spinoza in his first chapter
of the *Tractatus* definitely cites the marked differences
between his theory of prophecy and that of Maimonides.
The differences are clear: for Maimonides prophecy was
not only a fact in one book but also in reality, for Spinoza
it exists only in the Bible. According to Maimonides,
therefore, there can be prophets in all ages, and seeking
the cause for the lack of them in these ages in Israel, he
finds it in the oppressed condition of the people. For
Maimonides prophecy is not at all supernatural, but is
part of man's nature. Spinoza insists that the whole phenomenon of prophecy as it appears in the Bible is beyond
explanation. Spinoza therefore will not class the prophets
with the sages and thinkers, but places their activity in
the realm of the imagination. But Maimonides cites three
conditions under which it is thinkable that a man may
rise to the sphere of prophecy: perfection of spiritual
capacity, perfection of fantasy, and purity of conduct.
Of these three conditions Spinoza accepts but two, the
perfection of the imagination and good thoughts (*Tract.*
II, 10).

That Spinoza had the *More Nebuchim* open before him as he wrote is shown by the fact that he finds it necessary to discuss the word *ruach* which Maimonides uses in his argument. The latter says that *ruach* may mean the influence of the divine spirit on the spirit of the prophets (*More* I, 40), while Spinoza says that in the Bible *ruach* also has the meaning of imagination (*Tract.* I, 32 ff). Again we feel that Spinoza has the *More* open before him when he insists that Hagar had the gift of prophecy which Maimonides had expressly denied her because she was not possessed of the three conditions of prophecy. From these differences it is noted that Spinoza used practically all the data of Maimonides although he applied them for his own purposes. Furthermore, there is to be seen in the *Tractatus* an almost verbal borrowing of the thought of the *More*. Almost word for word does Spinoza use Maimonides' thought that the Jew referred all things as coming directly from God (cf. *Tract.* I, S and *More,* II book, chap. 48). Then Spinoza continues: "The revelation [to the prophet] occurs either through words or through images, or through both. These words or images were either real or were the phantasy of the prophet, since the imaginative power of the prophet even when he was awake made words and images so plain that he seemed to hear the words and see the images." (*Tract.* I, 9). These are the very words of Maimonides in *More* II, 36. Furthermore, Spinoza works out the explanation of the reason for the use by the prophets of similes and parables and the putting of spiritual truths in a material form exactly in the manner used by Maimonides. So we go through the whole *Tractatus* and find frequently almost word-for-word borrowings from Maimonides. In the fourth chapter of the *Tractatus* we read, "Under the human laws I understand the manners of living, which serve only for the protection of life and the state, while under divine laws

I understand those laws that regard only the highest good, true knowledge and love of God" (*Tract.* IV, 9). Maimonides says the same thing in the same words in *More* II, 40. Both Maimonides and Chasdai Crescas place the highest good in the love of God, exactly as does Spinoza. The vaunted *"amor intellectualis dei"* of Spinoza, the intellectual love of God, is announced centuries before by Maimonides in the last chapter of the *More Nebuchim.* So throughout the *Tractatus,* as shown chapter by chapter in the careful study by Dr. Manuel Joel in his *Spinozas Theologisch-Politischer Tractat auf seine Quellen geprueft* (Breslau, 1830).

It may be shown just as conclusively that the basic thoughts of Spinoza's system were taken from the *Or Adonoi* of Crescas, and that even the new thoughts in Spinoza's *Ethics* are to be derived rather from his attitude toward the philosophy of Crescas than from that toward the philosophy of Descartes. This has already been done in the remarkable study "Crescas and Spinoza" by David Neumark, which may be found in appendix of the eighteenth volume of the *Central Conference of American Rabbis Yearbook,* and I shall not even summarize this study as this paper is stretching out beyond my first intention. I desire only to point out that Spinoza employs exactly the same method of saving the omnipotence and free will of God that Crescas does, though Crescas (II *Trac.,* 3 sec., 2 chap. at the beg.) derives it from dogma of creation which Spinoza does not accept.

Finally let us see briefly how the very heart of Spinoza's whole philosophy, his theory of God, is based on Kabbala, especially as found in the *Zohar.* This theory as the basic thought of his *Ethics* may be worded as follows:

The only being is eternal matter, unlimited in time and undivided in space (for there is no emptiness in endless space),

41

all individual beings, including man with his intellectual capacity, being merely different modes of being, the appearances of which are the effects of the proportions of movement and rest within that unique matter bearing its eternal laws in itself [as formulated by David Neumark in his essay on "Crescas and Spinoza" in Vol. XVIII, p. 318 of *C.C.A.R. Yearbook*].

Now let us note how this pantheistic view appears in the *Zohar*, being sure that Spinoza knew the work as he was surrounded by mystics, among whom Manasseh ben Israel was foremost. In the *Zohar* we read (*Zohar* III, 65) "I am the true being, the inclusion of all being in All"; and Spinoza says, "There is but one Substance, absolute being." The Kabbala calls God *En Sof;* so does Spinoza call him The Unending. The Kabbala calls God *'ala D'alin;* so does Spinoza call Him Cause of all Causes.

The teaching of the Kabbala is that God is the Thinker, the Thought and the Thinking, made one in Him. The world is God's thought, so the world and God are one. It is the teaching of identity upon which Spinoza bases his pantheism too. In the knowledge of God, he says, "do we perceive after Him the world. For these are nothing else than one idea of God, which cannot be considered different from Him, the Absolute Unity." Spinoza distinguishes two attributes of God: knowledge and extension. God is the universal intelligence; He is the eternal absolute substance, there exists nothing that does not exist in His nature, or is outside His substance (*De Deo*, ed. Sigwart 6). And the *Zohar* says: The absolute intelligence is the cause of all being and cannot be removed therefrom. All is One, the Aged one (meaning the Eternal), outside Him is nothing. Spinoza writes (*De Deo*, ed. Sigwart 102, 103), The human intelligence is an outflowing of the divine, whose mode it is, and from which it arises; while the *Zohar* (III, 288) has it "Indeed, the

heavenly Wisdom is the earthly wisdom; this heavenly
or divine wisdom is secret and the cause of all other wisdom." "Except God there is no more substance, nor is
any thinkable," states Spinoza in *Ethics* I, 46, while the
Zohar (III, 288a) says, "All that exists is in Him, He includes all. He is the All." Among the thirty-six axioms of
Spinoza the twenty-eighth has it that "the cause of all
causes is the absolute cause, which is the cause of itself
and that is God. Through this relation of things all things
are bound up with one another and All is One. God, the
Universe, Cause and Effect are One." The same thought
is expressed by the *Zohar,* "God is the cause of all causes,
the creative cause of all things" (III, 299). "In the
Cosmos everything is bound up together, this with that
and that with this, so that we know that all is One. The
Universe is the Aged One (the Eternal) Himself and
cannot ever be separated from Him" (III, 290). Spinoza
says *Deus sive natura;* the *Zohar* says Nature is the God
of *Sabaoth,* the forces. In the thirty-sixth axiom of the
Ethics, Spinoza says that all that happens is not the play
of accident, but rather a consequence of Providence working in nature. And the *Zohar* (II, 100) states, "There is
no Accident." All, even the breath of the mouth, has a
purpose. "God is space," says Spinoza; the Kabbala calls
God *Mokom.* Ueberweg wondered (in his *History of
Philosophy,* III, 63) how Spinoza could explain *"causa
sui"* being the cause of himself. Spinoza's explanation of
this, found in his "Tractate on the Improvement of the
Understanding" is practically what the *Zohar* states: "God
is the First, the Cause of all Causes who Himself has no
cause. He is the Holy One (transcendental One), the
Old One (Eternal). He is the cause of all existence, who
exists in Himself (*causa sui*) and so is without cause or
origin" (III, 288). In a word the *K'la had* of the Kabbala
is Spinoza's "All, God and the World, are One." Spinoza's

pantheism was drawn from the teachings of the Kabbala.

Does this study, showing that Spinoza was of his time and of his people, degrade his fame or reputation or position as a great philosopher? It only tends to show that he employed the fine threads, scarlet, purple, and blue, of Ibn Ezra, Crescas, Gersonides, of Maimonides and the Kabbala, to weave a noble tapestry of God and Man and Human Blessedness, which has become the pattern of all the modern philosophies. To note the Jewish origin of these threads is glory to Israel, no less glory to Spinoza.

THE PRIMACY OF THE SYNAGOGUE:
HOW CAN IT BE RE-ESTABLISHED?

THE LONG ROAD of man's immemorial progress through the ages is strewn with the debris of discarded institutions. They were once conceived to meet human needs, to lift mankind over dangerous areas, to be a crutch to support some natural weakness or a shield against the siege of some imperious aboriginal urge; but there came a time when the need ceased, when man thought that he had mastered a situation and felt that all danger of being deflected from his upward march from barbarism to civilization by this or that obstacle had passed. Then he cast aside these once necessary agencies for his progress along the road to human perfection. No institution remains in use much longer than it is needed. Furthermore, institutions which were once of the first importance, because their function was imperative and crucial, gradually were reduced in rank as the need for them became less urgent. The law of natural selection prevails in this field as it is determinative in the survival of species.

With each people, a special institution stands forth as the outstanding one, holding primacy above all others because it best expresses that nation's soul. It is indistinguishable from the very life of the group, and if it lose its prime position, or be entirely discarded, the racial or religious entity of which it was the coefficient becomes inert and lumpish and eventually dies. The synagogue is the institution which holds such a primacy in Israel. It is

Paper read before the Central Conference of American Rabbis, Atlantic City, New Jersey, 1938.

45

the clearest and truest expression of the soul of our people and marks us not as a secular nation but as a religious community. If the Bible and Talmud are taken as criteria of the Jewish soul, then the central position of the synagogue in the life, aims, and goal of Israel stands assured. If religion is the all-important single factor in Jewish history, it follows that the dominant institution in every Jewish community is the synagogue. There are, of course, other and vital factors in Jewish life and Jewish story, but the synagogue stands for the principle of the primacy of Judaism in the drama of our people. The attempt to make Jewish culture or Jewish civilization central is a dialectic adventure marked by much confusion of thought and terminology, and, if persisted in, will prove to be only the first skirmish in an effort to displace religion from its commanding estate in our historic experience. A reaffirmation is needed at this time, in the face of the secularists among us, that Judaism was always and is still the most important factor in the life of our people, that faith and not philanthropy will save us, and that the voice of the synagogue has its vital message to bring to our people today, and to the nations that have forgotten God and His behests. If ever it was timely to reconsider the primacy of the synagogue and how, if indeed that primacy has been impaired, it may be re-established, it surely is pressingly so now.

However uncertain the data may be about the age of the synagogue, whether it had pre-exilic origins or rose in the Babylonian Exile or came into being during the Hellenic period, the character of the synagogue and the central position it held in Jewish life, at least from the year 70 A.D. down to the end of the eighteenth century, are fairly well known. During all these centuries it was recognized as the central Jewish institution, and though it comprised many functions which are now considered secular, it was inherently a religious institution. It was first and foremost the Beth Tefillah, the house of prayer and of Jewish liturgical devotions, but it was also the Beth Hammidrash, the place of Jewish study, and the Beth Hakkeneseth, the center of social relaxation and communal meetings. Needless to say the second and third functions were permeated by the spirit of the first. The synagogue was the central institution and all religious and communal effort radiated from it. There prayer and preaching, religious instruction and charity, weddings and other social functions were indulged in. It was the focal point of all Jewish interests and activities. Architecturally it was the most spacious and outstanding building of the community and usually stood above all other surrounding structures.

It seems that there can be no question to one who knows the history of the synagogue as to the primacy of that institution in the life of the Jewish people, a primacy that was obvious physically, culturally, and religiously and was never disputed. It was the beating heart of the Jewish people, the *beth ha-am,* as Jeremiah called it, the *beth moed* (Job). As Dr. Kohler in *The Origins of Synagogue and Church* says (p. 7), "The real dynamic and spiritual power, the fashioner and constant refashioner of Judaism in the various lands and ages was the synagogue." It was in the synagogue that the soul of Judaism became vocal and the Jewish people felt most at home. Naturally it took the central and primal place in the thought and activity of our people. It sprang into being to meet a definite need when the people had no Temple to which to repair, as in the Babylonian Exile, or when somehow the dramaturgy of the Temple worship did not completely answer certain spiritual yearnings of the Jewish soul. It rose not in opposition to the Temple, but as an informal supplement to the priestly liturgy, and almost wholly a laic movement and creation. As we know, this laic character persists to the present day, the rabbis being no hereditary priesthood and having no authority except as character and learning command it. Speaking of this institution Dr. Schechter in his discussion of Zunz's *Gottesdienstliche Vortraege* says (*Studies in Judaism*, Series III, p. 115),

Here you have the Synagogue as a living body with its two great institutions of praying and teaching. The prophets and the Soferim come, and when these disappear they are followed by the sages. New and mighty religions emerge which menace the Synagogue in its very existence, and it survives their attacks. New theories about God and man become prevalent which are rather hostile to Judaism, but Jewish philosophers understand how to assimilate them and enrich them by the treasury of ideas possessed by the Synagogue.... What now prevents us from building on this basis and from enlarging this treasury by the best ideas of our time for the benefit of posterity, as our ancestors did for us?

This "sublimest expression of Israel's life" has been the unquestioned authoritative and representative institution of the Jewish people in every city, town, and hamlet where at least a *minyan* of Jews could be found. That primacy and that title as representative of Israel has become somewhat clouded in the last 150 years, and recently has been consciously questioned and often entirely and cavalierly disregarded. The task of this paper is to consider a number of questions in regard to the gradual dethronement of the synagogue from its seat of primacy. How was the primacy lost, and why? Should it be retrieved? Can it be re-established, and how?

How did the title to the primacy of the synagogue become clouded? At least three factors in this process may be noted. The first and perhaps the most potent factor is the spirit of secularism, which encouraged dynamic personalities, largely recruited from the financially powerful elements, to accept the opportunities given them to be of service to their people, to usurp the authority of the synagogue, to acquire communal prestige, and to assume the representative function for the Jews resident in their district or nation.

Another factor in this displacement of the synagogue from its central and primal position was the increasing complexity of Jewish and general communal life, and the specialization of functions which it entailed. This is most clearly seen in the larger Jewish communities, where the philanthropic and social service programs became so extensive and required such expert administration that almost the whole enterprise of social ameliorative effort was removed from the precincts and even the direction of the synagogue. In many instances even the educational system of Jewish culture was taken away from the synagogue premises and its control placed in the hands of avowed secularists. As a result of that same growing complexity most of the community's social activities were concentrated in social and fraternal organizations separated from the locale and very frequently from the spirit of the synagogue. Where once the synagogue was the house of prayer, the school and the club, the hospice of the poor and the meeting place of all communal gatherings, its functions were taken away one after another until it remained principally a place of prayer and of preaching and teaching.

A third factor in this displacement of the synagogue from its central position was the attenuation of the cohesive force of Judaism in the Jewish community. A sweeping and radical congregationalism broke down and dissipated much of that influence commanded by the synagogue as a symbol of a united and commonly accepted tradition. Accompanying this breakup into religious groups was a deterioration of religious education and also of the dignity and standing of the rabbinate. All of these factors tended to reduce the synagogue to a minor place in common appraisal. Above all the prevailing secularism in the general community, the world at large, originating with and encouraged by the growth and prestige of the sciences, accelerated the movement and depressed the synagogue into a secondary, and in some places a negligible, position in the administration of Jewish affairs.

Can the early primacy of the synagogue be re-established, should it be re-established? Of course, it is out of the question to restore into the precincts of the *beth ha-am* the many diverse and enlarged activities and programs along educational, philanthropic, and social lines which in the last century have developed apart and away from the synagogue. They would not fit into the physical confines of that institution. The umbilical cord that once united the mother-synagogue with her various children has been severed and the progeny have grown. But the fact must certainly not entail a hostility or even a lessening sympathy and understanding between the begetter and the begotten. The spirit of the synagogue must pervade the philanthropies of the Jewish communities if a certain hardness and rule-of-thumb method is not to displace the Jewish warmth and brotherliness in social service processes. It must be the controlling influence in so-called Jewish education if a narrow secularism of blood and language is not to change the religious emphasis that historically characterized this important field. It must be present in the social activities if they are to escape ostentation, exclusiveness, and all their shoddy brood.

That this insistence on the primacy of the synagogue and of the religious point of view must especially be made at this time must be evident to all of us who note the unblushing acceptance in Fascist nations of the doctrine of the rightness of force and might and who see the unspeakable barbarities of the Nazis accompanied by the flouting of the teachings of mercy and justice which derive from the Ark of religion. As perhaps never before the Jew, who gave religion to the world, should be in the position to reaffirm the religious and moral obligations of man to man in a world that has lost the compelling vision of brotherhood and the gentle amenities. When the Divine is so deeply obscured as it is in our modern world, with the saddest consequences to the Jews and to all liberals and all minorities, our Jewish community must strategically reorganize itself that out of an authoritative synagogue the message of the Divine may have a revitalized force. We have come to realize that neither economics nor secular education will redeem us from the chaos and cruelty, the spiritual obtuseness and barbarism of this age. They have both failed miserably. It has not been the scholar in the universities of Germany and Austria who has stood up and protested against the barbarities of the Nazi rage; it has been the bearers of religion who have courageously sought to hold back the engulfing tides of paganism. Recognizing all this, we should make every effort to re-establish in the Jewish community the primacy of the synagogue.

How may that be accomplished? First and above all a long and candid process of self-criticism and self-scrutiny must be indulged in by those who are the protagonists of the synagogue. An appreciable increase in the efficiency of the synagogue must be effected in the conduct of those things which are its prime concern. In an age of crass materialism, it must be the spiritual mentor of the Jewish people. Its devotional elements must be reappraised, its liturgy must respond to every nuance of Israel's thirsting soul. It can no longer depend on impulses of devotion surviving from religiosities of the past. It must make a definite and strong address to the mind, but above all its emotional appeal and its spiritual content must be of the highest and most effective kind. The preponderant position of the sermon must be reduced, so that the devotional part will, at least, strike a balance with the intellectual and hortatory section. If the primacy of the synagogue is to be re-established, its educational program needs a thorough overhauling, with objectives more intensively taught, with a far greater amount of time alloted to them, and with the program offered to youth and adult groups as well as to the children. The synagogue must again become the schoolhouse of our people, so that some of the appalling ignorance of our literature and history and Jewish belief may be replaced by an enlightened and enlivened background as we seek direction in the maze of Jewish problems.

Any agency which aims at leadership must be ready and willing to take a definite stand on matters which fall within its field. And if social reconstruction and social justice do not fall within the sphere of consideration of a religious body, if the moral implications with which such questions are rife are foreign to such an institution, then we will have to formulate other definitions for religion. Social ideals are the very warp and woof of Judaism. The synagogue traditionally accepted such questions as its very own, and it should be unthinkable that of all the religious organizations which are vocal on social reconstruction, social security, social justice, the synagogue should be silent. If the synagogue thus fails in its prime function it has abdicated and deserves to be the fifth wheel in Jewish communal life.

Many are the questions in this field which are clear and well understood in their moral implications, and on these questions the voice of the synagogue should always be forceful and impressive. But while courageous utterance is demanded, so also are mature judgment and careful appraisal — and silence, when the moral implications are not clear and more light is needed. Complicated economic, social, and often political issues may involve many obscure factors which should make us hesitate before making magnificent pronouncement. Authority, dignity, and confidence become unraveled and lost through hasty and slipshod grandiose statements not founded on deep study and thorough knowledge and an appreciation of all factors involved. More and more must the synagogue participate in study courses on social problems and social reconstruction. Such courses will bring us more light, correct our position on related problems, and raise up in Israel a rank and file that will be ready to take an enlightened and firm stand on many a crucial social moral issue. Effective leadership in the synagogue will come only when the spiritual leaders and the body of the people stand together for righteousness in social relations.

If it is true that the synagogue has lost much of its influence because of dissipation of strength in internecine struggles between the various groups in the household of Israel, then our next step is obvious. To re-establish the primacy of the synagogue it is necessary to bring to some terms of co-operation those groups which have been too busy fortifying their respective positions against each other rather than against their common enemy, the secularism and the materialism that are rampant in the world and that stop at nothing in the way of cruelty and hate. The primacy of the synagogue may yet be retrieved if those who are of the synagogue, whether Orthodox, Conservative, or Reform, will rise above our admitted religious differences toward a union of the synagogue's religious forces.

To be sure, we have taken the first step in that direction in the organization of the Synagogue Council, in which

are to be found the accredited representatives of the synagogue from the Reform, Conservative, and Orthodox
groups. It might well become the voice of the synagogue
— the religious voice — speaking to the world as representative of that phase of Jewish life which is distinctive. But
much remains to be done to achieve for this Synagogue
Council the important place it should take in the life of
American and world Jewry. For one thing, its personnel
should be increased and be of a character, both lay and
rabbinic, commensurate with the importance of the Council in the enlarged ambitious program contemplated for
it as the voice of the synagogue. Then, of course, its
powers, now extremely limited, should be vastly aug-
mented and the terms of office should be considerably
extended, so that long-range plans may be laid down with
some assurance of continuity in the whole procedure.

The synagogue would then be in a position to assume
its old-time leadership; and the first task it would undertake would be to call for that unity in American Israel,
as it speaks to the world for Jewish and human rights,
which alone can make such protests and demands effective. To speak plainly, the synagogue, through the Synagogue Council composed of the representatives of the
organized religious life of the Jews of America, will demand that B'nai B'rith, Jewish Congress, American Jewish
Committee, and the Jewish Labor Committee shall join,
and once this is effected remain joined, with the Synagogue Council in a unified front before the world, a five-
fold front from which the characteristic religious organization of the Jew shall not paradoxically be absent.

Like any other institution the synagogue is enhanced
or reduced in power, prestige, and force of appeal according to the quality of the leadership which it commands.
The lay and rabbinic leadership must be outstanding in
character and ability, as well as enlightened and spiritu-

ally minded. A weak and petty and time-serving rabbinate means eventually a despised synagogue, while a learned, able, and selfless rabbinate exalts it. Thorough preparation in Jewish learning and right character, in addition to a careful appraisal of other less obvious but at least equally important factors, should be the basis upon which decisions should be reached as to ordination for the Jewish ministry. The official bodies of our congregations should be advised as to the crucial importance for their congregations and for Judaism itself that wise choice be exercised for their religious leaders, that congregations may be protected against those who, without preparation, and at times without the requisite learning and character, seek their pulpits.

Then, too, we must do what can be done — and it seems with the right spirit a great deal can be done — to limit the number of those who desire to prepare for the rabbinate according to the number of pulpits likely to be available. For a fierce competition in the rabbinate such as exists in commercial life will without doubt have a very deleterious effect on the morale and character of the Jewish ministry. A careful study of the status of the rabbinate, which was planned some years ago by the Central Conference of American Rabbis, should immediately be initiated on as thorough and broad a scale as possible. And in consonance with the results of such a study, measures should then be adopted to mitigate some of the unfortunate conditions which seriously affect the rabbinate and the primacy, indeed the effectiveness, of the synagogue.

Among these unfavorable conditions in the American rabbinate, two will be found of a very serious nature, both of them affecting the morale of the rabbi and his usefulness for all that the synagogue stands for. One has to do with what is now generally accepted as the normal and just right of all workers, namely, social security. A very considerable number of our colleagues are receiving salaries that preclude a decent standard of living, while the large majority of the rabbis see no chance of setting anything aside for the time of sickness or old age, or for the eventuality, which is always before the ministry, of loss of pulpit. We have been entirely too dilatory in the matter of creating, as similar groups in the Christian church have done, some sort of pension system or old age insurance. Let us think just a little of our own household when we speak in ardent support of social security. It involves not only the security of the rabbi but — if we realize the effects of insecurity upon the daily task — the primacy of the synagogue.

The second situation which seriously militates against the dignity of the rabbinate, and hence against the effectiveness of the primacy of the synagogue, is the chaotic and almost anarchic condition in the matter of pulpit placement. With the large and ever increasing number of rabbis, without a corresponding increase of available pulpits, we are witnessing an exaggeration of what always was a deplorable system of pulpit manipulation. When, for instance, even a modest pulpit becomes vacant or is rumored to be so, a sort of undignified "gold rush" of applicants appears, followed by wire-pulling of all kinds and climaxed by the horror of trial sermons. It is not the intention here to blame the individual rabbi, who naturally seeks to advance in his chosen profession; it is the system that is responsible in the extreme. We wonder what remains of respect for the rabbinate after a congregational bout with half a hundred anxious and often hard-tried applying rabbis. It is a most undignified scramble for pulpits, and in the course of it, through the years, much of the primacy of the synagogue has been lost.

If we are at all desirous of re-establishing the primacy of the synagogue or even of improving the lot of our colleagues and preserving our self-respect, we dare not say, well, it has always been so. Nor can we hope for some situation to arise of itself to do away with this morally devastating system. Nor can we be satisfied to point out that the system referred to is atoned for by the absence in Jewish life of a hierarchical form of government. Something must be done speedily to change matters in pulpit placing. Orderly pulpit placement which would avoid a stampede of applications and which would provide that promotions go to those who on their record deserve advancement, that the needs of a congregation be recognized, that it be supplied with a rabbi whose qualities are known to fit the situation — that is the problem. Is such a thing possible? Well, there are denominations which manage this kind of pulpit placing with the preservation of the dignity of the ministry and without undue hierarchical pressure.

In this connection it may be suggested that the whole subject of Synod deserves to be again carefully explored, not perhaps in all the phases for which it was projected before our Conference in 1903, when in the President's Message there was reference made to "the lack of a central authority . . . with regard to ecclesiastical matters," but with the object of meeting the situation referred to, while at the same time guarding the autonomy of the congregations. The Synod was before our Conference as a practical question through the years 1903 to 1906, and the discussions centered about the possibility of establishing an authoritative body in our Conference to keep down some of the theological aberrations in our congregational life. We hardly think that the adverse vote on that question reached in 1906 would be changed now.

Perhaps the name Synod with its special historical connotations should be discarded, but certainly there may be devised some form of rabbinic and lay organization — committee or bureau, if you will — of wise and just men chosen from different sections of our country, who without further ambitions to fulfil as to their own advancement, will study the needs of each congregation whose pulpit is vacant and will be in position to nominate a rabbi to the congregation through a knowledge of his fitness and of his right to a promotion. Such a Pulpit Placing Committee or Synagogue Consultation Bureau — composed of rabbinic and lay members — would make impossible the unholy scramble and wire-pulling, would give encouragement to men to serve well in small pulpits in the knowledge that advancement would come according to the ability proven, and would at any rate reduce the acerbities that develop in congregations during the fevered period of filling the pulpit as the process is generally conducted even by congregations which are supposed to know better. Such a bureau, properly districted, might be helpful in adjustment of differences between rabbis and congregations, and rabbis and their colleagues.

The Central Conference of American Rabbis has boasted of the fact that it is now not only the largest organization of rabbis in the world, but the largest in the history of Israel. Is its influence commensurate with its numbers? If we seek to re-establish the primacy of the synagogue, let this largest rabbinic group assume its responsibility and demand that it be recognized as at least equal with those other groups that speak for American Israel. Let us solemnly take our stand on important questions, but let us not bury our conclusions in our Conference Yearbooks. A wholehearted process of publicizing among our own congregations the statements and decisions of the Conference should be developed by the different committees of the Conference. Every Jewish newspaper, every Jewish opinion-forming agency should be supplied with official digests of Conference activities and studies and pronouncements. Let the voice of the synagogue be heard above the Babel of the other voices that claim to speak for the Jew. Printer's ink should be more assiduously used by the Conference, far more than has thus far been done, for the enlightenment of our people as to a definite Jewish approach both to our peculiarly Jewish problems and to world-wide issues.

To be sure, most of what has been here outlined is but organizational, the mechanics necessary for the rehabilitation of the synagogue as the prime institution of Israel. We have here the stark derricks and winches, the levers and fulcrums, as it were, for the lifting of the *beth ha-am* back to its rightful place in Jewish life. To give this machinery due attention in one way or another is imperative at this time, otherwise the authority and usefulness of the synagogue will be further seriously impaired. But beyond and above all this, something else must take place in the Jewish scene, an inner transformation without which all this machinery will be but ambitious parade. "A new heart and a new spirit," for which the prophets of old always pleaded, must be created in the synagogue or we die as effective messengers of the Lord of Hosts. The underlying and transfusing element of the synagogue must be again soundly and roundly spiritual, with all the hard grit which has filtered into its sacred precincts from the brittle materialism of the surrounding world entirely removed.

A legend current in Brittany tells of a "cathedral under the sea" submerged by the enchantments of a stranger knight who had opened the floodgates with keys put into his hand by a wilful princess. Because faithful souls still kept vigil and prayer the cathedral under the sea remained intact, while implacable waves pounded and battered it and the briny waters bit deep into its walls and pillars, until one day it rose from the sea while its bells tolled as of yore its living message to a long unhappy world. So has the synagogue been submerged, as some enemy of the people opened the floodgates of a secularism and materialism alien to the Jewish spirit; and as happened before, human arrogance and selfishness swept imperiously through the sacred shrine, drowning out the voice of religion. The briny waters have invaded not only the synagogue but all the hallowed homes of the spirit. If only we of the synagogue, lay and cleric, keep prayerful vigil, if we will not allow the flood tide of secularism to batter down the pillars of faith or the corrosive waters of a Godless philosophy to demolish the holy of holies; if we will only hold fast to the spiritual ideals and values which are the Jewish heritage, the synagogue under the sea of a world-wide devastating flood will rise again to bring living teaching and a message of blessing to our people and to mankind.

The burden of this high task rests heavily upon our shoulders as rabbis in Israel. It was inevitable that some of the sea change which the synagogue's submergence wrought should come upon us. The wonder is that so few of us have sought acclaim above all things, have compromised with evil, have fled Jonah-like from announcing unpopular messages of God, have aimed at worldly comfort and place and applause instead of rejoicing in our task even in lowly and humble positions. Yet all of us must be reinvigorated spiritually. The synagogue under the sea, the submerged synagogue, will be raised only if a "new heart and new spirit," unbitten by the prevailing tides of evil, are created in those who stand and serve in the precincts of the Lord. The magic of Jewish conviction and selfless devotion to the spirit of Judaism will lift the synagogue to that place in Jewish life where it will again be the heart and center, the abiding hope and the motivating theme of a people dedicated these thousands of years to truth and righteousness and human brotherhood.

When all is said there are just two ways of re-establishing the primacy of the synagogue: first, by making the synagogue worthy and capable of accepting the responsibilities that go with primacy, a synagogue which supplies the needs of our people in the social and religious and moral spheres, through a lofty spiritual service and an enlightened, free, and capable rabbinate; and second, by insisting vigorously that the synagogue has the right of representing the Jewish people, has the right of directive influence and leadership as of old. The synagogue, lay and rabbinic, will through these methods displace modern secularism and assume again its primacy.

THE NEED OF A NEW IDEALISM

SINCE LAST WE MET in annual convention, the dogs of war have slipped their leash and, for eleven months now, have bitten into furious madness one half of the civilized nations of the world. The fiercest, largest, and least excusable war in all history is being waged across the sea. Civilization, culture, religion — all are forgotten in this almost universal return to the heritage of the cave man with his club and his stone. All the fine restraints of the ages have been dropped into the seething cauldron of national hate and greed. The blood-red trail of Mars is easily traced all over the map of Europe. Millions of men have been drummed together from peaceful homes and occupations, have been equipped with the tools of destruction, and have been set over against each other for mortal contest. A hate that they never felt has been artificially nourished in their breasts, so that in the day of combat the beast in them may override the human being. And in the ensuing conflict, large sections of the most beautiful provinces of France and Poland have been scarred beyond recognition, great monuments of ancient and glorious architecture have been wantonly destroyed, homes have been ruthlessly demolished, lives have been mercilessly sacrificed, and coming generations have been saddled with a burden of debt, physical, moral, and financial, that will draw the sweat of the masses of men for a century to come.

And as we from the outside contemplate this darkest

The Lecture delivered at the Central Conference of American Rabbis, Charlevoix, Michigan, 1915.

blot upon the escutcheon of civilization, we fail to find a single noble excuse for this welter of blood and agony of hate. No great cause rears itself above the blood-stained standards of any of the contending nations; but instead, the bait of greed for land and power and commerce shows itself on every hand. There is nothing in it all to give it even the hint of glory, no great rallying cry for freedom, no appeal of the oppressed, no rousing bravado of a tyrant of men. It is a contest of the market place, a mean squabble over the fleshpots; and all that makes a tragedy of what would otherwise be the most laughable farce is that the coin with which the price is paid is compact of blood and tears, of quivering, shattered limbs and agonized hearts. To be sure, some memory of earlier protestations of humanity has caused the nations to produce their white and blue and yellow books, but when all the leaves have been turned and their contents digested, we come back to the first impression that they are but fine feathers to cover the nakedness of a very brutal body of greed.

Is it any wonder that people the world over are thinking sadly of the dreams of yesteryear? Is it any wonder that the spiritually minded in all lands are discouraged at this fatal collapse of the program of civilization? Many there are who do not hesitate to call it the bankruptcy of religion. They see the hollowness and futility of religious teachings of peace and good will, of righteousness and humanity, which bring only a fruitage of hate and greed and the sword; for you cannot long keep people from noting so clear a break between profession and practice. Among these, religion will have a harder task than ever before. They will either turn away permanently from such unproductive doctrines, or demand a sounder, solider, and more compelling restatement of the postulates of religion. They will either mock and sneer at the sorry farce of a religious program that breaks at the first strain, or insist upon a deepening of all the founts of faith. Religion will have to reach into the depths of being and become so completely a part of self that not even the fiercest upheaval will reveal a fault and effect a cleavage. The mere veneer of faith, the lip service of religion, will not any longer appeal to this generation made sadly wise by blood and burdens and suffering.

If the teachers of religion across the waters will have to take account of this new wisdom and this novel and earnest insistence upon a solider and a finer faith, we on this side of the welter will almost equally be put upon our mettle. A more impressive and a more cogent presentation of the faith that is in us will have to be made to gain anything like the acquiescence that our earlier statements obtained. There should be many, too, among us who will anxiously ask themselves, if at all worthy of their high office, whether their teaching did not lack something of the right fervor, whether their reasoning did not fail in something of cogency, and whether the philosophy back of their preaching was not as halting and as materialistic as must have been that of many of the European teachers. Analyzing the collapse of civilization in Europe, we will come to realize that the prime cause of it all is the fatal cleavage between the philosophy that guides the common life and is its background, and the religious doctrines which have with little or no change been repeated for ages. There was no harmony between the philosophy of life and the philosophy of faith. And if we would save our land and our people from the frightful experiences which are saddening the homes of Europe, we must bethink ourselves with renewed solemnity of the duties incumbent upon us as religious teachers.

Emerson in his cryptic way says that there are times when the priests are wooden and the chalices are golden, and there are times when the priests are golden and the chalices are wooden; meaning that in some periods of history the priests themselves are humble and self-effacing and the doctrine they teach is pure and precious while at other times the teacher vaunts himself and reaches out for worldly glory and pomp and the teaching is wooden, dead and uninspiring. If ever there was a time when the chalices of the priests of mankind should be golden, their teachings all-compelling, it is now when the times are out of joint and the madness of hate and the insanity of blood are in the air. If ever there was a time when the teachings should be pure and precious, it is now when the blatant and defiant materialism of a half-century is reaping its Moloch harvest. Now at the culmination of a period of Aladdin-like revelations in the physical world, of wonderful utilitarian discoveries, and of marvelous victories of inventive genius, now when these remarkable triumphs in the world of the senses have raised Positivism and Practicality to their apogee, is the time for the golden chalices. Now when the lust of the flesh, the lust of the eye, and the pride of life have transformed into mere opportunists men and nations who, half a century before, had been enthusiastic idealists engaged in movements that were sweeping civilization upward as well as onward — now is the time that the priests become self-effacing while their doctrines ring true with a newer note of faith recalling the olden spirituality.

The more so is this change a peremptory need of the time, since the crass philosophy of positivism and the gross materialism of the second half of the nineteenth century have not passed by the man in the pulpit. He, too, has lent his ear to its tone of promise for a revelation of the mysteries. He listened ardently while the monism of Haeckel presented to him, with all the modern scientific paraphernalia, a "vibrating ether" as the beginning of things; an attenuated, light, elastic jelly endowed with sensation and will, "though in a very low degree," and he was asked to bow down to this jelly-god as the ultimate cause of all phenomena. He heard other scientists claim as much or more. Tolstoy reported that a learned professor had said to him that "all the faculties of the soul have now been traced back to mechanical sources; only consciousness is not yet explained," expecting, of course, that it soon would be. Think of it, "only consciousness," as if that was but an incident instead of being the very crux of the problem; yet so positive and self-confident had the materialistic investigators become. And this certainty on the part of the scientists could not but impress the teacher and the moral leader. Thus we find H. G. Wells baldly stating the corollary to all these confident claims when he says, without any conditional clause: "The history of a nation is the development of its external resources." Historians, economists, and moralists adopted the same hard tone, and might and glitter and force were acclaimed anew as they had been in the darkest day of Rome.

And as for us in the Jewish ministry, well, you may remember we were told not so long ago that this growing and terrible materialistic monism would wash the very ground from under our feet, that it was sure to leave us stranded if we did not change the character of our preaching. To be sure, he who thus warned us had not gotten so far away that he could brazenly ask us to preach what was the natural consequent to his thesis, the doctrines of a Nietzsche and his group; instead he gave us a program of protest, a program of negativism. With one hand he swept away the old preaching of the spirit, the old enthusiasms and the ancient bending low to the God of our fathers, and with the other, so that Othello's occupation be not gone, he gave us a semipolitical task of protest against the growing spirit of sectarianism. To such a prospectus of protest did materialism reduce the moral thunderings of the prophets and the devotional soarings of the psalmists and seers!

Even before this gratuitous advice had been given to us, many of us, in the conflict of doubt that the revelations of science had stirred up within us, had turned away from *'Abhoda* as a futile farce and had thrown ourselves, as though to save our self-respect, into *Gemiluth Khasadim*, social service. There, at least, we felt that we were on sure scientific footing, that we were helping in the world processes instead of standing by and muttering fatuous incantations. We became known and active in every movement for social betterment in the community; instead of rabbis we were efficiency experts, tenement house reformers, scientific charity advocates and agents. We had turned away from the soul and were busied with the body of the community, the "physical resources" in which H. G. Wells found all the glory of a nation. Across the waters many nations are learning in tears and sorrow that along that road of philosophy are bitterness and agony and death.

But even before the brutal scourge of war brought people to their senses, a change had come over the face of the philosophical world. Just as in nature there is ebb and flow, going and coming, systole and diastole, so positivism was giving way to idealism, egoism to altruism, material ascendance to spiritual domination. Sir Oliver Lodge's statement is borne out by the facts when he says: "Haeckel is abandoned by the retreating ranks of his comrades as they march to new orders in a fresh direction." Hans Driesch, a prominent biologist, insists that "the mystery of the vital forces is being increasingly emphasized by nearly all leading biologists." Bergson and Royce and Eucken are the new and acclaimed leaders of thought.

The French philosopher offers the inexplicable *élan*, a sort of divine push, as the start to the world phenomena, while Royce and Eucken are presenting to the world, with ever increasing force of argument and logic, their doctrines of idealism. Listen to Royce:

And despite the vastness, the variety, the thrilling complexity of life of the finite world, the ultimate unity is not far from any of us. All variety of idea and object is subject to the unity of purpose wherein we alone live. We have no other dwelling-place but the single unit of the divine consciousness. We are eternally at home in God.

These men, not in ignorance of the results of science, but rising through and above them, thus posit the unity of the divine consciousness. And with them the Neo-Kantians, with Hermann Cohen and Rueckert in Germany and Muensterberg in America, are repeating the chorus, "the world is fundamentally ideal."

With this new wine the golden chalices are being filled. New, yet old, for it is the wine of Socrates and Plato, the wine of the prophets who sang to the refrain, "The grass withereth, the flower fadeth, but the word of our God stands forever." We must raise this new chalice of gold before the eyes of our people, forgetting the old doubts and the cooled spirit. We must follow the course suggested by our teacher of the third century, B.C., and accept the aids he proposes in the order he gives them. Our program must be Knowledge, Worship, and acts of Benevolence. Knowledge must be first, and we must seek truth wherever it may be found, not fearing anything, even science. Somewhere in our search we will come to the place which Tennyson reached when he said:

> Flower in the crannied wall,
> I pluck you out of the crannies,
> Hold you here, root and all, in my hand,

Little flower — but if I could understand
What you are, root and all, and all in all,
I should know what God and man is.

We must seek the truth until we are thrilled to cry out
as did the Psalmist, "The heavens declare the glory of
God and the firmament proclaims His handiwork"; we
must look with keen gaze all about us until the wonder
strikes into our very being and we exclaim with the
astronomer, "O Lord, I think Thy thoughts after Thee."
It is through knowledge in all its thoroughness and completion that man is forced upon his knees, and 'Abhoda
follows swift upon Torah. To make that 'Abhoda more
than a mere fixed duty, more than a sop to the unintelli-
gent, is our function, and, unless we have prepared ourselves by wonder and prayer and meditation, we shall not
be able to fulfil that function. Only by the avenue of
adoration and humility can we reach the high place of the
priest at the altar; only by personal spiritual exaltation
can we attain the Holy of Holies. Only then will our
services be rescued from dead decorum into a living spirituality. Then will come back to our freezing congregations the ardor of spontaneous song and praise, and irre-
sponsiveness and smugness will vanish before the spirit
of the Lord. Then the old messages of the prophets will
not sound like false echoes in our modern temples, but
will thunder with the old-time positiveness and unfalter-
ing conviction, as firm as the everlasting hills. And then
it will be the inward urge that will send us to our fellows
in social service not as a program of science, but as a
psalm of brotherhood.

This is the golden chalice that the times hold up before
us, containing the only wine of salvation for a much-tried
world. Professor Muirhead speaks of "the strenuous idealism of the Hebrew mind"; surely this idealism is not

dissipated. Let but the leaders return to the old paths of reverent spirituality and they will find the people waiting eagerly to be led into the ways of peace. Let but the spirit of idealism be wafted over the dry bones of an Israel that has in many respects become dead and inert through smugness; let but the leaders pray the praise and proclaim as did the seers of old and Israel will rise up an exceeding great host, mighty in the serene life of trust, humble before God and man, whole in body and soul, and enthusiastic in the service of brotherhood.

GOETHE AT ASPEN, COLORADO,
AND HIS DISCIPLES

DOES ONE NEED to apologize to the Critic Club when he introduces his paper by a Biblical quotation — even if it is from so nontheological a section as the Book of Proverbs? At any rate I take the risk, and quote from King Solomon, or from some less wise and not so much-married author who may have written in part or whole this Polonius-like list of moral and prudential admonitions. Says this unidentified writer, "There are three things which are too wonderful for me, Yea, four which I know not,"* and he repeats this formula a number of times in chapter 30. So, in the same manner, I might give three, nay four, reasons why I have chosen the theme of "Goethe at Aspen, Colorado" for discussion at our Critic Club.

The first reason is one of vicarious pride in that the Critic Club has the distinction that two of its most honored and worthy members were among the directors of this great bicentennial Goethe celebration, under the honorary chairmanship of Herbert Hoover, and the chairman and president, Robert M. Hutchins of Chicago University. They are Dudley K. Woodward, Jr., and Karl Hoblitzelle. Through them, we and all Dallas have been honored by their sponsorship — in a fine company of similar noble spirits — which made possible the exceptional Goethe Convocation and Music Festival from June 27 to July 16, 1949. The second reason for my paper

---

Paper read before the Critic Club of Dallas, February 20, 1950.

*All Biblical quotations are from the Jewish Publication Society of America Bible (Philadelphia, 1917).

is that it is always well to remind ourselves of our debt to the great Titans of world literature, Dante, Shakespeare, and Goethe, who attained the very summit of Olympus, and to attempt to reappraise them and their messages to their own generation and to ours. A third reason is that our modern world — our America among the other nations — is in the direst need today of the Goethe outlook, the Goethe dream, and above all the Goethe wisdom.

I regret that I have to cite a fourth and very unpleasant reason — namely, the suspicion that has come to me that many Americans may be in the class of one of our most esteemed journalists, Elmer Davis, so designated by no less a fellow-journalist than Edward R. Murrow in his 1950 New Year's Day mention of our modern "greats." For Elmer Davis, newscaster, journalist, author and one-time "Voice of America," wrote a brief letter in the October issue of *Harper's*, stating that in his opinion Harold Ross, who was born in Aspen, Colorado, is a far greater man than Goethe, the "stuffed shirt" born at Frankfurt, Germany, and unduly honored at Aspen. When I wrote to Mr. Davis at his Washington, D. C. address asking him to enlighten me about this Harold Ross — who no doubt is a fine gentleman, but who must be hiding his light under a bushel not to have received in a more general way the honors reserved to anyone who was greater than Goethe — I received quite promptly the courteous answer that Harold Ross was the editor of no less a weekly than the *New Yorker*. I learn from my son that the *New Yorker* is a bright weekly magazine, slanted to appeal to sophisticated people. So Harold Ross, originally of Aspen, Colorado, is far greater than that "stuffed shirt," Johann Wolfgang von Goethe! The Bicentennial Convocation and Music Festival was certainly needed, and it is hoped served as a corrective to such denigrating appraisal of a great poet, novelist, and dramatist, and wise governmental administrator.

I had hoped, when I chose this subject for my paper, that the promised volume of the papers that were read at the Bicentennial by Albert Schweitzer, philosopher, theologian, and physician — and musician — founder of the hospital at Lambarene; by José Ortega y Gasset, humanist critic and philosopher; by Robert M. Hutchins; by Thornson Wilder, novelist and dramatist (who read his paper on July 5, at the session over which Dudley K. Woodward presided); and by many others would be available for my study in time for the preparation of this paper — but up to the moment of writing the volume has not appeared. So, in this appraisal of Goethe, I had to go back to the sources — which is in itself a good discipline, and puts the onus of my appraisal where it belongs, on my own head. I hope when the volume of the Bicentennial does appear I shall not be found too far off the track.

Let us first consider the man, Goethe, apart from his literary work, apart from his message to his time and to ours. Wordsworth contended that no one should pry into the private lives of authors; "our business is with their books — to understand them." But there are those who, on the contrary, urge that the fullest understanding of books requires some fairly definite knowledge of the life of the author and the times in which he lived. A leading London neurologist, Dr. Walter Russell Brain — appropriately so named, it seems — has been curious about the psychic condition of great writers, and reported in a recent issue of the *Journal of the British Medical Association* about some medico-literary autopsies which expose the mental instability of many a genius. Some great writers, according to Dr. Brain, were insane in the strict sense "that they would today have been regarded as certifiable."

Others, although not certifiable, were manic-depressives, obsessionals, alcoholics, or drug addicts. John Donne, for instance, had a morbid obsession with death ("Never seek to know for whom the bell tolls; it tolls for thee") which prompted him to pose in a shroud for the sketch of his own monument. Dr. Brain insists that Jonathan Swift in his *Gulliver's Travels* shows evidence of a mind "emotionally arrested at an infantile stage of development." And in the same way he offers case histories of Samuel Johnson, "the great convulsionary," obsessed with a sense of guilt and fears of insanity and death; of James Boswell, a manic-depressive, whose brother and daughter went insane; of Charles Dickens, with his periods of excessive elation and depression blended with sado-masochism — a sex perversion in which man derives pleasure from inflicting pain or from suffering pain or humiliation at the hands of another — the marks of which run "like a scarlet thread through all his writing," especially in the unbridled violence of *A Tale of Two Cities*. And along with these, among the mentally sick writers of all nations, Dr. Brain includes Baudelaire, Dostoevski, Flaubert, Poe, Rousseau, Strindberg, and Goethe. And as Dr. Brain concludes his studies of genius we learn the end of the matter is that no man is a great and creative artist because he is a psychopath; but, if he has the other necessary qualities of mind and spirit, the element which many psychiatrists would call pathological may be essential in his genius.

That Goethe had some pathological elements in his nature — and who has not? except thee and I, and sometimes I believe that thee has them too — anyone who runs through the two volumes of Goethe's letters, selections from his autobiography of the first twenty-six years of his life, and excerpts from the reminiscences of his friends and acquaintances, published in 1949 by Ludwig Lewisohn, will in all likelihood agree. From these hundreds of letters, autobiographical details, and reminiscences we learn that at a very early date in his boyhood he was somehow obsessed by thoughts of grandeur; his mother tells that he would often gaze at the stars, of which he had been told that they had been favorable at his birth, and would anxiously say to her, "Surely the stars will not forget me, but will keep the promise they held out over my cradle." Again his mother reports that when he was seven years old he said, "I can't get along with what suffices other people." He was a strange child, his mother remarks, as she tells of standing at the window with a friend as the boy, Wolfgang, was coming up the street with other boys with a grave and dignified air. When he entered the room the mother's friend teased him and asked why he bore himself thus. The young Wolfgang answered, "That is only the beginning; later on I will distinguish myself in quite other ways." In his autobiography he writes of his youth: "All this time it was undoubtedly in my mind that I was to bring forth something extraordinary — and the symbol of it was to be the laurel wreath which is meant to crown the poet."

The manic-depressive reactions, as also those excessively excitable and violent, are found in many incidents told in his own letters and autobiography — *Poetry and Truth (Dichtung und Wahrheit)*. When Gretchen, his first love, slipped out of his life when Goethe was but fifteen years old, we read in the autobiography, "When still, from time to time, the pain over the loss of Gretchen renewed itself within me, I would suddenly weep and lament and bear myself in an unruly fashion." Then at Leipzig, where he attended the University, he writes that his passion for Annette was at its height — and then tells of "the tears which she shed over my misbehavior and I was in great dismay." He admits in his nineteenth year

that he brought with him from home "a certain hypochondriac tendency," and in cheerful company he was
morose. From time to time throughout these two volumes
his friends and even casual acquaintances write of his
excessive excitability.

His relations with women were violent and fitful, from
Gretchen and Annette and Lotta and Lilli Schoenemann
— to whom he was once formally betrothed — and Mari-
anne von Willemer and Charlotte von Stein, to Christiane
Vulpis, who lived in his home in Weimar from November
1789, bore him a son in August of that year, and was duly
married to him August 19, 1806. In speaking of their relationship, the poet Schiller said, "Unfortunately, through
false notions of what constitutes happiness and through
an unhappy nervous fear of marriage, he has slid into an
entanglement which oppresses him and makes him
wretched in his very home and which he is too weak and
too soft-hearted to shake off." But as Goethe himself said,
"She has always been my wife." Madame de Stael speaks
of "the contradictions of his character, his moodiness, his
embarrassment, his reserve, which are but shadows at the
foot of that mountain upon whose peak his genius has its
place." Even Christiane confesses, "I am much worried
about him. He is sometimes quite a hypochondriac, and
I have to put up a lot with him." Well, if all these symptoms make Goethe psychopathic — then aren't we all,
though we may not be geniuses?

But let us note his other traits. A stranger, a student,
writes to him of his problems, his difficulties, his aims,
and his deficiencies, and straightway Goethe asks him to
come to the University of Jena, hard by Weimar, where
he will obtain for him a lodging and give him an annual
pension. The pension amounted to one third of his own
income, as Privy Councillor to the Duke of Sachsen
Weimar. His request of his physician to use a considerable

sum of money which Goethe entrusted to him for needy patients and never to mention the name of the donor is along the same lines and is the pattern of his frequent benevolences. Says his friend, the poet Schiller, in a letter to a countess:

My friendship with Goethe I still, after an interval of six years, regard as the most beneficent in my entire life. . . . It is my profound conviction that no other poet comes near being his equal in depth and delicacy of feeling, in nature and truth, and at the same time in the high perfection of his art. No more gifted man has arisen in the world since Shakespeare. . . . And it is to be remembered that he has used the greater part of his life — more than 50 years, in fact — to perform the duties of a minister of state which have been neither small nor insignificant because this Duchy [of Sachsen Weimar] is small. Yet it is not these singular merits of his spirit which bind me to him. If his human worth did not seem to me to be the highest among all men I have known, I would have been content to admire his genius from afar. But I am able to say that in the six years of our intimacy no slightest doubt of his integrity ever arose. He possesses the highest veracity and sense of honor and the deepest earnestness in the pursuit of what is right and good.

When he was presented to Napoleon and had conference with him, the hero of Austerlitz said of him, "Voilà un homme." Surely we must agree, there is a truly great man.

But why should the 200th anniversary of the birth of Goethe be so signally and dramatically celebrated as it was at Aspen, Colorado? Let us consider first the drama of last summer, and then set forth some of the reasons for the celebration, with reference to the need for our own country, for Germany, and for the spirit generally prevailing in the world at this time. In the green valley west of the towering mountain peaks of the Continental Divide, with the brawling, torrential waters of Roaring

Forks running through it, the town of Aspen grew swiftly during the silver rush of the turbulent 1880's which began with the assassination of President Garfield by Guiteau. The valley was fringed by vast aspen and evergreen forests and walled in by the high Rockies, a setting of unspoiled natural beauty. But this did not protect it from the fate of becoming almost a ghost town when the price of silver sharply declined, unsupported as is the custom nowadays by federal government arrangements. Later the town was revived as a skiing resort with incomparable slopes and perfect snowing conditions.

An outdoor amphitheater was Nature's added gift to make Aspen an ideal setting for the Goethe Bicentennial Convocation and Music Festival. A spacious platform with a vast tent ceiling was provided to protect distinguished speakers and artists from wind and weather. In these dramatic surroundings the bicentenary of the birth of the devotee of nature, the *grand seigneur* of German literature, was celebrated from June 27 to July 16, 1949. Here for two weeks philosophers like Albert Schweitzer, José Ortega y Gasset, William Ernest Hocking of Harvard; educators like Robert M. Hutchins, Chancellor of the University of Chicago; novelists like Thornton Wilder, recipient of three Pulitzer awards; historians like Ludwig Lewisohn and Rev. Edward A. Walsh, S. J., Vice-President of Georgetown University; and poets like Giuseppe Antonio Borgese of the Universities of Milan and Rome, and Stephen Spender, all set themselves to study and analyze the style and message of the man whose poetry Coleridge and Carlyle proclaimed to be without equal in its loftiness of thought and beauty of rhythm, to whom Byron dedicated two of his plays and whom he called the greatest genius of the era of Encyclopedists. Adding to the glory of the celebration, world-famous artists and orchestras offered recitals of selections from Goethe's over three thousand poems, set to music by Schumann, Hugo Wolf, Schubert, and Beethoven; and the Minneapolis Symphony Orchestra under the direction of Mitropoulos played symphonies, concertos, sonatas, and overtures by Brahms, Beethoven, Mendelssohn, Wagner, Bach, Mozart, and Liszt.

Why now are we called by this bicentenary celebration to turn back to the man born in the middle of the eighteenth century who lived on for eighty-three years through the first third of the nineteenth century? Said Robert M. Hutchins, the chairman of the Board of Directors of the Goethe Bicentennial Foundation:

It may be impertinent to celebrate our own recognition that the human spirit which he apotheosized, is the locus of our difficulty. We are not gathered here in an antiquarian or academic mood; still less in a sentimental. We are gathered here to search out in ourselves the depths of the spirit that sustained the optimism of Goethe. If he had reason to be optimistic, we have need. We need his spirit more than he did.... It is a World Convocation and a World Festival, for the difficulty of our time is a world difficulty, and the spirit of Goethe is a world spirit.... Where we ride madly on the torrent of the present, dreading to raise our eyes or turn our attention, Johann Wolfgang Goethe stood astride the current, astride it, not apart from it.

We are to ask ourselves: What has Goethe done to make us better — or rather what is that within his life and writings which might help us better to meet and solve the problems that beset the age and each of us of this age, two centuries after him? To reach some reasonable conclusion we should have clearly before us the bare items of his life and its works: He was born at Frankfurt-on-the-Main, August 28, 1749, attended the University of Leipzig 1765-68, and went to Strassburg in 1770, made the acquaintance of the sonnets and plays of Shakespeare, and at the university took his degree as a doctor of laws. He practiced rather unwillingly and desultorily in his profession, but employed his time and found his finest satisfaction in poetic effusions. In 1773, when he was barely twenty-four years old, he wrote the drama, *Goetz von Berlichingen*. In 1774 he published *The Sorrows of Werther* which made him world-famous.

In 1775 Goethe accepted the invitation of Duke Carl August of Weimar to come to his service. He became a councillor in charge of roads and of mines, and later was for many years director of the Weimar theater, remaining in that service all his life, toward the last in an honorary capacity. The Italian journey, which marked an epoch in his life, took place in 1786-87 — almost the exact middle of his life. *Faust: A Fragment* appeared in 1790. The novel *Hermann and Dorothea* was published in 1797. The first part of *Faust* — as we now have it — appeared in 1808; in 1816 the poet was at work on his *Autobiography* and his *Italian Journey;* the first part of *Wilhelm Meister's Apprenticeship* appeared in 1821, and it was completed in 1829. The complete *Faust* — first and second part — was finished on July 20, 1831. Goethe died at Weimar on March 22, 1832, after he had said, "Open the blind of the other window, so that more light may come in."

Carefully appraising this great and varied mass of literary work, one critic answers the question, What has Goethe done to help us better to meet the need of the age?, by pointing out that he has taught us to aspire and endeavor to be no fragment of manhood, but a man. He has taught us that to squander ourselves in vain desires is the road to spiritual poverty; that to discover our appropriate work, and to embody our passion in such work and such toil must not be servile, but glad and free; that the use of our intelligence must not be chiefly to destroy, but to guide our activity in construction; and that in doing our best work we incorporate ourselves in the best possible way in the life of our fellows. Such lessons, the critic, Edward Dowden, says may seem obvious, but they had not been taught by Goethe's great predecessors of his age, Voltaire and Rousseau. Goethe, unlike Voltaire, inculcates affirmation — not negation — and urges reverence and love; unlike Rousseau, he teaches us to see objects clearly as they are, he trains us to sanity. Thus, in the *Sturm und Drang* (Storm and Stress) period of Europe in which Goethe lived, he could not find it in his heart to side unreservedly with the French Revolution, however much he sympathized with the hungry and angry masses that stormed the Bastille. The outbreak of the Terror, its official proclamation, the avid and undiscriminating guillotine conflicted with his orderly sense of justice, with his sanity, with his zeal to build and his hatred of destruction. In the year 1790 he wrote in his poem "From the Venetian Epigrams,"

> On France's ill fate let the great beware,
> But let the humble have an equal care!
> Yes, the great fell. But who protects the mass
> Against the mass, which its own Tyrant was.

In *Hermann and Dorothea* he reveals his capacity to treat with justice even those of whom he could not approve intellectually, and to find noble motives in actions with which he could not be in accord. Behind the clash of political passions he uncovers the eternally human; with marvelous skill he depicts simple family life — which is the chief staple of humanity and civilization — caught in a social upheaval which seemed to drive men to devour each other. Hence as a minister of state at Weimar, as a theater director, poet, philosopher, natural scientist, discoverer of the intermaxillary bone, elaborating the new theory of man's origin which has led many

to call him a percursor of Darwin, he could not be for
the Revolution and the Terror and the guillotine. For
him not the Revolution but evolution through education
— more and more light and more and more humane spirit.
: All of this has relevance in our day and time. Though
the social order has been rearranged, the old evils appear
under new names. Literacy has flourished, but taste has
been debased. Goods have been produced and produced
in untold quantities and blown up by bombs — atomic
and the less destructive kind — in untold quantities.
Things seem to be bigger; they do not seem to be better.
We are face to face with the fact that our difficulty, like
the difficulty that Goethe apprehended in his day, is not
primarily political, economic, technological, but is the
difficulty of the human spirit. His disciples, like Albert
Schweitzer and the long list of distinguished scholars and
philosophers who brought to Aspen their thoughtful and
warm tributes to his memory, were impelled to emphasize
this spiritual difficulty which faces our time in America,
in Goethe's own Germany, and in all of Europe and the
world generally. Many thoughtful people here in the
United States and in Europe and Asia have come to sense
something of that spiritual difficulty of the age.

. This feeling comes to us as we face the puzzling situation that in these years when science is king, and highly
esteemed, practical Americans are so much interested in
Gandhi and Schweitzer, religious mystics. It may be that,
whatever the dominant climate of opinion, men and
women are glad to hail in the presumably self-seeking
world such personalities as Gandhi and Schweitzer who
demonstrate how it is possible and necessary that some
persons can and do honestly pursue aims much more to
the credit of our human powers. Yes, they are religious
mystics — if you so wish to term them — but they did not
take their stand away from life, like Simon Stylites, upon

a pillar removed from the turbulence of our common existence. One faced the spiritual dilemma in a subcontinent, to be felled by the bullet of a political assassin; the other faced the diseases of central Africa, the separation from the culture he loved, and the consequent deadly boredom which oppressed him all too often, in order that he might solve his spiritual difficulty by healing the humblest and least considered of God's children and building a hospital among them.

Such mystics we need, whether they find their inspiration like Gandhi in the Rig Veda and the personality of Gautama Buddha, or like Schweitzer in the complete Faust story and other writings of Goethe, or in the Bible, Jewish and Christian, and the personalities of an Isaiah, a Hillel, or a Jesus. But besides the religious mystics we have the historians and poets and philosophers who tell us of the need of the world today in terms of spiritual insight. They point out that the German people, of whom Goethe came, need it sorely today. Thomas Mann, who wrote *Faustus*, tells them that they accepted a path which "caused their millennial history to be invalidated, reduced to the absurd, and has proved by the event to have been an accursed aberration and mistake and brought it thus to issue in chaos, in despair, in an unexampled bankruptcy, in a descent into hell, around which flames of thunder danced." In this long aberration and secular sin, said Ludwig Lewisohn, Goethe had no share. A moderate conservative, a lover of the best, of quality, like most authentic artists, he looked with sharp distrust and prophetic shame upon even the earlier, more pardonable and more amiable manifestations of German separatism, of German arrogance, upon the whole German cult of pride and blood and soil and sword. It should not be hard for the German people to read in Goethe's books and in his life the lessons of remorse, contrition, and expiation; for him who ever strives upward through all his errors there is redemption in the end. Then Germany's difficulty of the human spirit will be surmounted.

Goethe is the universal spirit personified. Germany did not confine him, nor Weimar, nor the Swiss Alps, nor the genial Swiss people, nor sunny Italy which warmed him so in the exact middle of his life and renewed his creative spirit. Beyond all these lands he looked to Greece and its calm classical beauty; and, at the same time, to Persia and Hafiz and Hatem and the spirit of romance which he caught in his *West-East Divan*. He was interested in faraway America, in a book of travels which tells of the celebration in Philadelphia of the important anniversary of William Penn's first arrival in the New World, and he asks for further information about a "curious colony inhabited by a variety of Quakers, who call themselves Shakers," which the traveler reached on the road between Boston and Albany. And in 1821 he indites this poem "To The United States":

> America, thy fate is kinder
> Than that of our old continent,
> No ruined keeps are thy reminder
> Of ages misspent.
> They soul is not shaken
> As thou buildest thy life,
> Because there awaken
> Old cries of vain strife.
>
> Use then thy fortunate present so
> That when thy children come to write,
> A kind fate guide them to forego
> The false romance of ghost and knight.

Of England he thus speaks to Eckermann, the Boswell of his latter years: "The Englishman seems to have advantage over others whom we see at Weimar. What handsome, able fellows they are! The good fortune of personal liberty, the consciousness of the English name and the significance attached to it among other nations — these accrue to them even in their childhood. Within their families and at their schools they are treated with much more respect than children are elsewhere, and thus they enjoy a happier and freer development."

It is this universal spirit which we need in our day — if the United Nations or One World is to mean anything toward solving and surmounting the difficulty of the human spirit which we face in this period of the cold war.

Dr. Hutchins speaks of Goethe's optimism which should be emphasized and followed in our day. Reading his writing will bring reborn encouragement as we note how in his time a great mind met the challenge of disillusionment. The latest Nobel Prize in literature went to T. S. Eliot who has been telling us that modern life is a wasteland, and the only thing we get from him is moral defeatism. When in 1832 Goethe finished *Faust*, he had lived much longer than Eliot has yet done, and in a period of huge upheaval, perhaps greater than, certainly as great as that which we and Eliot have witnessed. Born in 1749, he had lived through the Enlightenment, the turmoil of the American and French Revolutions, the disturbing adventures of Napoleon, the return of the Bourbons, the dislocations and disorders of the Industrial Revolution and the uprisings of 1830. What effect did these seemingly catastrophic happenings have on Goethe? How did he outlive them both in years and in outlook? We can read it all — disillusion, sickness of soul — in the greatest of Goethe's works, *Faust*. And let us remember what many forget, that *Faust* as a drama has two parts — and though the first part is the better known it is not the greater part. Faust is Goethe himself: he chose the old legend of Dr. Faustus as a basis of his poetic drama, because he found in it intimations of his own soul, and his own spiritual development was therein recorded far beyond the intention of the medieval author or authors of the ancient legend.

The first part of *Faust* might be called the "Tragedy of Margaret." It ends in the violent death of her mother, her brother, and her own and Faust's baby — and in her legal execution after her reason has left her, and after Faust departs with Mephistopheles. It begins with Faust dissatisfied with dry, dead book-learning, and in that mood he accepts the bargain offered by the Devil, a very suave person, outwardly a gentleman, but really the spirit of cynicism, the Everlasting No, looking down, not up, and seeing in man's ideals nothing but mockery — "the spirit that always denies." The bargain which Mephistopheles offers is that he will bring Faust the joys of life which his dry books in his dusty study failed to achieve for him, but Faust's part in the wager is the agreement that when in his search for life's pleasures he comes to feel such superlative satisfaction that he is impelled to cry out, "Tarry, O moment, thou art so fair!" (Verweile doch, du bist so schoen!) then he forfeits his soul to the Devil. From the beginning of the bargain the Devil is sure that Faust with all his fine emotions and yearnings will gladly eat "dust"— triviality, carnal pleasure, and evil. And in so doing, Faust destroys Margaret — though he himself through remorse and repentance, and by the power and appeal of the eternally feminine — *das ewig-weiblich zieht uns hinan* — which purifies him, still has not forfeited his soul. He has another chance.

That chance comes in the second part of *Faust* — the chance which came to Goethe after his boisterous years of romancing — the chance which comes to everyone, but which not everyone grasps. Mephistopheles takes Faust to the imperial court and has him try his hand at political power which proves unsatisfying, for politics, he finds, is a tricky business which often plays up misleading patriotisms. Mephistopheles even induces Faust against his better judgment and conscience to persuade the emperor to inflate the currency — you note the temptation is also modern. After other experiences in political power and in aesthetic creation, all of which fail to satisfy him, Faust chooses finally what may seem a huge anticlimax in his search for happiness. He now is an old man and blind. But he elects to redeem a tract of wasteland from the ocean.

What is it that is appealing enough to this man who has tried everything to induce him to this final effort and to find in it such real importance? The fact is that on this new soil, redeemed from the ocean's grip and saved from the wasteland, Faust sees a new type of civilization arise — a world of free men and women, winning their freedom for themselves and maintaining it by efforts ever fresh, banishing from among them the hags of Want, Blame, and Crime. In that fruition of simple creative work Faust finally finds complete satisfaction and cries to the passing moment, "Stay, thou art so fair," and the time has come for Mephistopheles to claim his soul. But in this very aspiration after the perfect joy of others — not his own — Faust is forever delivered from the Evil One. The gray old man lies stretched upon the sand. Higher powers than those of his own will take him, guard him, and lead him forward. The messengers of God bear away his immortal part. "The soul which strives unceasingly can be redeemed." So ends this great mystery play. Overcoming the skepticism of Voltaire, and the natural loves of Rousseau which lead to Margaret's death, and eschewing the lust for power and the false aims of politics, ever striving toward some simple creative work which will bring satisfaction to self by achieving the happiness of others, Faust

— Goethe, you and I — is redeemed. That teaching is the supreme lesson which Goethe teaches this age to surmount the difficulty of the human spirit. That, it appears, is the justification of the Goethe Bicentenary Celebration.

SERMONS

MEDICINE FOR A SICK WORLD

And the fruit thereof shall be for food,
and the leaf thereof for healing.

Ezek. 47:12.

THAT THE WORLD OF NATIONS is very sick is so obvious a fact that few thoughtful observers of the course of contemporary affairs fail to note it and fewer would dare to deny it. It is not any sort of inherent pessimism which prompts people to pronounce that the world is stricken with a serious illness; it is only what honest observation — the seeing eye — reports to us. Only the other day a prominent publicist called attention to this sad condition of human affairs. He is not a pure academician who is annoyed at the noise of the world intruding upon his much-beloved cloistral quiet. He is not one of the so-called unpractical men who are alarmed at the normal grind of the wheels of life, startled at the clangor of its regular noisy machinery — and who, in terror of the hurly-burly, prophesy the advent of the doom of nations. He knows all the chicaneries of diplomacy, and the devious ways that have been taken by nations to obtain their ends throughout the course of time. And it is this man who, in the very midst of the international tangle of things, accompanied by total war, puts his finger on the world's pulse and says that there is a fever of a serious nature in the body of society today. The world is sick — almost unto death.

Well, from time to time, the political and economic and spiritual doctors have discovered a sick world, and

December 8, 1940.

we imagine the world has been more or less ill from some trouble or other at every stage of its development. There seems to be nothing new, then, in ferreting out maladies among the nations of mankind. But what is interesting is the remedies which from time to time are suggested and prescribed. You know many of the remedies with which we were overwhelmed by Townsends, Upton Sinclairs, Coughlins, Fascists, Nazis, Communists, silverites, militarists, and pacifists—their number is legion. And each is certain that if you only adopt his plan — be it the Epic or the Share the Wealth, be it limitation of armaments or ruthless war measures without end, be it economic control or the controlled rubber dollar — if only you give his scheme a chance to prove itself, the world will be healed of all its sickness.

The prophet Ezekiel in a sort of parable — for he is the one prophet who most loves to speak in pictures — tells us of his suggested remedy for the troubles of the world. In chapter 47 of his book he speaks of a river whose "waters issue forth toward the eastern region, and shall go down into the Arabah" — and every living creature in the stream shall live and thrive — and every field that it waters shall flourish with a new strength and fertility. What does this healing river mean? Wherein lies its power of regeneration, of renewal of strength and virility? What is the secret of the "river of healing"? I find the secret in the few brief words of verse 12 of this chapter 47 — the secret of the healing power is revealed in the words, "Because the waters thereof issue out of the sanctuary." In plain words, the prophet Ezekiel feels certain that the ills of society — in his day or any other day — can only be cured by spiritual means — *out of the sanctuary*.

So, too, the great modern publicist, Francis B. Sayre, speaks concerning our modern ills. He shows that during the past hundred years we have been living through a

92

period of unprecedented material development and progress. New and undreamed-of power was generated by the
creative inventions and ideas of the nineteenth century.
We made ourselves masters of the material world, but
there was clearly something that we lost in this conquest
— something most vital for human happiness. And that
something lost — that fine thing that we allowed to slip
out of our grasp as we went reaching for material gifts —
has taken its vengeance on us. The results speak for
themselves. A cataclysmic war which again drenches the
whole world in blood is count *one*. The economic catastrophe of the last decade — without parallel in history —
is count *two*. It is not honest thinking to regard these as
visitations of God which we are powerless to prevent.
They are clearly of our own making — the result of a social
and economic order which we ourselves have built up,
founded on the acquisitive instincts and making for social
injustice and economic insecurity. With all the material
mastery attained in the conquest of the forces of nature,
this generation has proven its utter ineptness to get the
best out of life, to discover its lasting happiness, and to
free it from the thousand confusions and disruptive movements which are endangering western civilization.

From an ancient and a modern seer we bring you the
verdict on all this malaise. Says Ezekiel, the prophet who
spoke in Babylon some 2,500 years ago, we need the river
of healing issuing "out of the sanctuary" which shall bring
life along its entire course, reviving the tree of human
idealism so that its "leaf shall not wither, neither shall
the fruit thereof fail." He calls for the healing waters of
the spirit to set us again on the paths which lead to the
fullest satisfaction and happiness. Mr. Sayre has the same
verdict, and calls for a similar cure. He says we have not
found the way to win and make secure the enduring and
really precious values of life. We have become essentially

a materialistic civilization. We have sought happiness
through acquisition. We have placed our ultimate reliance
for security on material things, material force. We have
largely ceased to utilize the matchless power and strength
that come through religion. We have failed to advance
in our comprehension and understanding of spiritual
realities. We are losing our faith, and with it our sense
of spiritual direction. We have acquired prodigious material power without a corresponding spiritual understanding and restraint.

Here we have the verdict — and the suggestion of the
medicine for this sick world. Many of us are in the mood
to take the medicine offered. The world is recoiling from
the disastrous effects of the gross materialism which has
followed our loss of faith, and the great masses of humanity are yearning now, as seldom before, for surer foundations upon which to build. There is only one way. From
widely shifting beliefs and differing faiths we must sift
out life's verities of human experience.

What are these eternal verities? May I suggest just a
few. They are not my own subjective personal pronouncements; they are the conclusions of history. One that all
history teaches on perhaps every page is that self-seeking
and self-indulgence, unrestrained, ultimately lead to suffering. These may seem to be the roads that lead to the
fuller and more abundant life — but they have proven a
thousand, thousand times to be utterly deceptive. They
have not only failed to bring happiness of any lasting
quality, but have become in every instance bitter on the
tongue and have left nothing but heartache and sorrow.
Another eternal verity is that dishonesty, whatever the
apparent gain today, inevitably undermines confidence,
and saps the possibility of rewarding relationships tomorrow — the relationships that lead to self-respect and trust
and a sure dependableness which the world is ardently

looking for and anxious to recognize and bow down to. The third eternal verity is that force and violence, however they may seem to gain quick results, destroy the very foundations of social security and thus ultimately delay the march of human progress. And finally, there is the eternal verity that understanding and love have more potency to achieve lasting results than material force or than hatred and hatemongering and racial and religious prejudice. These are the spiritual values, the saving teachings of all religions. They are religion, for they recognize a divine center, which we call God, to all our yearnings and strivings — a moral mortar holding together our universe.

The river of healing, we may now be sure, is not to be found in more inventions and scientific discoveries, though these will continue to be made, nor in improved methods of manufacture. These things will not stop heartache or broken lives or suicides. It will be found in spiritual values, such as inner happiness unconquerable by outward circumstances, joy in daily work and satisfaction even in commonplace labor, the affection of a chosen few and the respect of all, and some objective of existence which colors all life with beauty. These values, that cannot be built on material foundations, will be discovered to be the medicine we all need, for which we are all groping.

And we had better begin the treatment soon — taking this medicine to a sick world now. For every great civilization of the past has had its rise, its noontime brilliance, and its gradual decline into the sunset. How about our own civilization? Will it be free from this general deterioration? All we can do is to wonder — and try to save ourselves and our civilization from the dangers that we have the vision to see and the courage to attack. And such a grave danger besets our civilization today. The time is at hand, it would seem, when we must commence a new chapter of forward progress or watch a slow decline. The outcome — whether it will be advance of our civilization or a slow descent — depends not upon blind forces outside of our control, but upon ourselves.

Further progress — as against deterioration — demands building anew upon spiritual foundations. The one solution — the one medicine for this sick world — lies in the teachings of religion. In them is a power which can heal us all from this malaise which has resolved our civilization into dictatorships and panicky economic and financial experimentation, into supernationalisms and hypermilitarisms, into crusades of hate and into suicides of despair. In religion is the power of healing from all of this, if we are ready and willing to take the medicine. Religion — spiritual values — not more ritualism, not more ecclesiasticism, not even more dogmatic theology, but brotherliness, understanding, love, and self-sacrifice. The enduring values must become our measuring rods, the spiritual must become superior to material imperatives; above mass production, and dollars, and modern inventions, above the pride of our airplane and radio and television must come the reverence and humility before our God-given personality, before God and truth, justice and righteousness, brotherliness and love.

Reverting to Ezekiel, the prophet of the Exile, unless we allow the river of healing which issues out of the sanctuary to regenerate our lives — then our civilization will become, as the prophet describes in verse 11 of chapter 47, miry places and marshes and shall be given over for salt. Another dark age will then sweep over our proud lands even as it swept once over Egypt, then over Assyria, and then over Greece, and finally over Rome. The Vandals will again be at our doors — they are nearly there now. The same miry places, the same marshes of noisome growths will arise with us as they did in decadent Rome — and we "shall be given for salt," utterly dead and sterile as human beings and as a civilization. But if we turn our backs to this insistent materialism which demands all from us, and has gotten pretty near all it demanded, and if we bring spiritual values and religious demands into our life, and forget our vaunting at this wonderful, yet oh so pitiful skyscraper civilization, if we eschew greed and force and might and assassination and hate and irresponsible decadent spiritual thriftlessness, if God again will come into our human arrangements, if the voice of religion will again be heard in the land, then there will flow the river of healing bringing life and vitality, instead of boredom, suffering, and death. Then — again as Ezekiel suggests in another place — we of this modern age, in this valley of dry bones, with the breath of God again in our nostrils, will rise up a mighty, happy, godly host.

THE QUEST OF THE AGES

MAN IS the only discontented creation of God, and no doubt God intended to make him so. In the human breast there has been implanted what has rightly been called a "divine discontent." One poet has celebrated this quality of man's nature in the following lines:

> The thirst to know and understand,
> A large and liberal discontent;
> These are the goods in life's rich hand,
> The things that are more excellent.

For "from the discontent of man the world's best progress springs"; really this divine discontent "is the first step in the progress of a man or a nation" (Oscar Wilde). A similar thought is suggested in a beautiful legend found in the Midrash, the edifying stories of the Rabbis of old. They said that at dusk on the sixth day of creation, just when "by the word" man was to be created, the angels to their consternation discovered that all the materials for the creation of man were ready except that by some mistake the materials for the heart of man had been overlooked. God ordered them to seek such material amongst the fragments left over from the other days of creation. When finally the angels brought to God their finds of the leftovers, it was discovered that there were the pride and pomp of the lion, the ferocity of the tiger, the cunning of the serpent, the meekness of the lamb, the heat of fire and the cool of the glacier, the glow and warmth of the sunshine and the glint of the rivers. The mixture of these God looked at and felt its inadequacy for the heart of man, so He added love and He poured in hope and desire and covered it all with charity.

This is the heart of man, and the hope and the desire for joy and the better life — the very soul of discontent at things as they are — is the sustaining quality for human progress. This element of hope and desire makes man a questing animal; it sends him out on the quest of the ages. Each age sees man in some chapter or paragraph of that adventure of seeking. In the early days it was pictured as the quest of Prometheus, seeking fire from the altar of God to make warm and bright the cold and gloomy haunts of primitive man. And it may be added here, that as a symbol of the travail and never-ending agony of the human quest, none is more to the point than Prometheus, bound to the rock while the vultures gnaw at his vitals. The first quest is therefore for fire — that is, for warmth and glow and comfort and at-homeness in this strange and often hostile-seeming universe. Then the next quest of man which we meet is the search for the Bluebird of happiness, of which Maeterlinck tells us, but which is the mark of many ages; a quest which goes out to many far and foreign and strange places in the search for the Bluebird, only to come back home and find the Bluebird at one's own doors — for with the right spirit and keen vision happiness may be found very near our own hearthstone.

Later man tires of war and war's alarums and advances beyond the limited loyalty to his own family, with every outsider not of his group as his more than potential and in all senses real enemy — and the quest for neighborliness is begun in human history. It records itself first in the maturing heart of man, then later in his codes — the first being in the Levitical code found in chapter 19 of Leviticus, Thou shalt not defraud thy neighbor, shalt judge him in righteousness, shalt not stand against the blood of thy neighbor, and ending in that fine climax, Lev. 19:18,

"Thou shalt love thy neighbor as thyself." Long has been this quest for neighborliness, the neighbors increasing as the world gradually became drawn closer together by the development of the means of communication, until after the World War with fine courage and a trust and faith in man's better self which at times these days seems to have been quixotic and unfounded, the League of Nations was formulated. What is that League but a grandiose extension of the simple "Love thy neighbor" of Leviticus? And so the quest for neighborliness goes on (assisted by every move, halting and slight as it is, such as that to begin a year's armament holiday today. May that holiday extend to the end of days — then the quest would be finished!).

But alongside this quest for neighborliness, the kindly quest of lonely souls looking for a fuller completion by junction with humankind, is the hardier and ruder and more insistent and continuous quest for power. Throughout the ages the chieftain — Bedouin sheik or bandit leader — lifted himself above the herd by the urge of the quest for power. Through that quest family and village groups were organized under a leader and then developed districts under a military ruler, and then nations came, and kingdoms, Czarisms, Kaiserdoms, and empires. In that quest stand out the great military chieftains, the Pharaohs of Egypt, the Shalmanesers, the Nebuchadnezzars, Cyrus, Darius, Alexander the Great, Caesar, Napoleon, and our modern dictators.

In another way the quest for power has taken a different and far more blessed turn, for the quest for power has also sent man to leash the powers of Nature, to harness the lightning and to utilize the Niagaras. The modern scientist is pursuing the quest for power — power over our environment, power over noxious germs, power over devastating flooding of rivers, power over droughts by conservation, power over distance — yes, even bridging the distance of the millions and billions of miles in space to some far-off galaxy of the heavens. This quest gave us the telescope, the telephone, the radio, it gave us antiseptic surgery, it gave us merciful anesthetics, it is giving us immunity from typhoid and diphtheria and smallpox, it has given us Hippocrates and Galileo, Koch and Pasteur and Ehrlich and Lister, and Faraday and Nikola Tesla and Edison — to mention only a few of the great captains in that army of power that is marching to conquest over our environment.

But the underlying quest of which these are but polaric outshoots — favored in their successive rise by some strangely kind and strategic advantage — is the quest for the meaning of life, for the meaning of all the urges that send humanity a-questing, the meaning of the fire quest, of the neighbor quest, of happiness and of power. It resolves itself concretely into the quest for God, and this is the real quest of the ages, of which all the others are but facets and aspects, fragmentary and unsatisfying because they allay but one of the many thirsts of the human soul. The quest for God seeks to allay them all. "Everyone that thirsteth, come ye to the water," cried Isaiah, the great prophet, and he means "the water that is God."

It was the ancient quest, it is the one enthralling quest of the moderns — even though they know it not. It was the ancient quest, for then early man saw a god in every tree, as an individual and distinct divinity; there was a god in the sun — a very great god, perhaps the greatest — a god of the storms and of the rains and of the harvest — and they tried to appease these manifold gods, so that life might be made livable to them. The approach of the early man to God or the gods was only through some ritual — magic or sacrificial — through which their favor was to be gained.

It was changed as a quest very radically by the teachers and prophets of Israel who appeared between two and three thousand years ago on a narrow strip of land to the east of the Mediterranean Sea on either side of the Jordan. The meaning of life, while not fully explained, had come to be dimly understood by them through their finding the God of righteousness as the beginning and the end. The thousand riddles of human existence could be at least partially answered by the announcement of the Holy One. The problem of evil, while not fully explained by the prophets in announcing God, was somewhat clarified by the belief that God was all-good, and that evil was but the shadow of good. And they wooed their God of righteousness — these prophets of Israel — not through sacrifice, for they said that God hates sacrifices and is wearied of them, but by the good life, by letting "justice run as water and righteousness as a mighty stream," by "doing justice, loving mercy and walking humbly with God," by feeding the hungry and protecting the fatherless and the widow. In short, said these prophets — an Amos and a Hosea and an Isaiah and Jeremiah and Micah and the rest — God doesn't want you to do things for Him but for man, and if you live the right life with your fellow-man you will find godlike satisfactions, and you will find that therein and therein alone exists holiness.

Then came the medieval quest for God. It was really fraught with despair of the world as it is, for it sought God away from the world — away from the haunts of men, away from the very places where the prophets of old said you could find God. These medieval searchers of God sought him in solitude, in monastery and nunnery, in renunciation and asceticism. The medieval quest ended in some saints, truly saintly folks, but the kingdom of

God was not very greatly advanced through its search.

And now comes the modern quest. It is the search of God in nature, in history, in the very heart of man. It follows Him in the footsteps He has made in earth-strata, in suns and stars, and it finds the immensities of space appalling in their unthinkable quantities and distances. It follows Him through all the fields and laboratories of science to the very soul of man, the threshold of human consciousness, the conscience, the dim yearnings, the intimations of immortality — all that psychology is revealing. The modern quest for God is gently lifting the veil, pushing back the vast clouds of ignorance — and to the discerning mind discovering an even greater God than anyone ever dreamed.

To be sure, in the bright light of the new science many have become blinded so seriously as to miss God in the whole transcending revelation, but to the more thoughtful every step in the drama of modern science is toward unification — *one element* — at least, one pattern; every step is toward a mighty purpose, every step toward a vast and glorious design, leading inevitably to a great Architect of the universe. This Architect is announced by Professors Eddington, Millikan, and Jeans, amongst the very leaders in the quest, and also by thousands of the lesser lights. And so the quest goes on — through the ancient, medieval, and modern world — a search for the good life, a search for God. As they quested yesterday, so they will tomorrow — for human life is a quest, a divine discontent, a search for things unknown, for problems ungrasped, for power over Nature, and finally over self. May we also feel the divine discontent — may we follow the quest — applying to it that same earnestness and thoroughness and vision we use in the fields of the material advance of civilization. In that quest earnestly pursued, it may be that we will find God — perhaps still somewhat dim to our failing human sight, but yet recognizably God — the God of goodness and justice and of an unbounded mercy and love. And having found Him, we will love Him and live as He would have us — not for Him but for the finer, wider, happier, and more satisfying and completing life of our fellow-men on this spinning earth of ours.

STANDING IN THE WAY:
REST FOR THE SOUL

THE MESSAGE OF RELIGION is always the same, but different times require different emphasis on the various sections of that message. Wartime is always a time of severe tension, of fierce excitement, when twitching nerves are atingle. We rush from one thing to another, from one distraction to another; we are afraid to stop — we mustn't let our thoughts overwhelm us. So we submerge them by activity — of any kind, as long as it keeps us from thinking too much or too hard or too long. Wartime and this running along with the excited crowd, that thought might not intrude to trouble men too much, prevailed in the time of the prophet Jeremiah. So he underlined one needed part of the message of religion and said to his generation: "Thus saith the Lord: stand ye in the ways and see, and ask for the old paths, Where is the good way, and walk therein, and ye shall find rest for your souls." The writer of the classic book of Job felt that his generation needed a similar emphasis and admonition for he urged them: "Stand still, and consider the wondrous works of God."

This is the one effort we need in this hurried and harried age, that we might halt in the rush of things, to consider, to rest, and to meditate, or just to loaf. James Harvey Robinson, in his book *Mind in the Making,* and other psychologists have recently shown us that truly creative thinking takes its source in daydreaming, in that woolgathering process which is looked down upon by our efficient age as mental loafing. The need of the age

---

February 20, 1946.

is to stand in the ways, to stand still and consider, to ruminate and reflect on the astounding and disturbing events in which the present generation finds itself immersed, that some modicum of light may be shed on the road we must daily traverse. How can this be done? Let us set aside part of the crowded day, a single hour, a prayer or meditation hour, when, removed from the noise and haste and pressure of the world, we may turn in on ourselves, discover our inner self and the deeper currents of life and God's works. Such an hour, daily, or even fifteen minutes, would be a blessed release, comparable to the wonderful poet's hour:

> Once I met an angel by the way,
> A brief hour he stayed and then did part;
> And now his halo gilds my every hour,
> His song sings always in my heart.

It is the angel of the deeper insight, of the slower and truer understanding, the angel who interprets to the listening heart of man the cryptic and crabbed letters which this hurrying, worrying time writes upon the tablet of life. I speak for the angel of introspection, the angel of the quiet, the angel of the unfettered, unhurried, unharried soul. The angel of that hour might gild our every day and his song sing always in our heart. It is a silent hour, like the hour of the turning tide. Have you stood on the shore of the sea and seen the waves with hoary manes ride in and break with terrific din? There comes a moment of silence when these self-same waves, drawn by the lunar pull 238,000 miles away, turn about and with the same crash of sound with which they came in now ride out again to sea. That moment of silence is the turning of the tide; so the silent hour in our day, the hour of retrospection, the hour of thinking it all out, is the true turning of our life's tide. In that hour we hear the voice

of God, in a world that in Wordsworth's phrase is "too
much with us."

Once I was privileged to be present when a great
artist was seated at the keyboard of a majestic organ and
played as only an artist can. All the anguish and ambition
of life, its travail and querulousness and hopelessness,
sounded through the terrific crashes of the organ, until the
very air trembled. Then the great musician closed all the
stops, and pulled out only one that before was unused. A
sweet, tremulous, appealing note as from the very skies
soared in, and the spirit of a wondrous peace came over
us. It was the *vox caelestis*, the heavenly voice amidst the
reeds and basses, amidst the querulous high notes and the
sinister low thunderings. So in the midst of our life's vast
diapason comes the sound of the *vox caelestis*, at the silent
hour of standing still, when we consider the works of God.

And as in the silent hour we hear the voice of God, so
also do we discern the hand of judgment. That hand once
appeared in Babylon:

> The king was on his throne,
>   The satraps thronged the hall;
> A thousand bright lamps shone
>   O'er that high festival
> In that same hour and hall,
>   The fingers of a hand
> Came forth against the wall
>   And wrote as if on sand.

And the words that ghostly hands spelled out for the
king and his reveling guests to read were the fateful
mene, mene, tekel, upharsin — weighed and counted and
found wanting. This we come to learn in the quiet hour,
when we are free from the pressure of doing, and when
we stop to "consider the works of God."

Stand still and consider, stand in the ways and see!

How like the familiar warning at our railway crossings, intended to stop the headlong traveler hurrying to his destruction. We drive blindly with foot on the accelerator and with the brake off, toward the many fatal crossings of life. And then we wonder that so many of us are crushed beyond recognition by the oncoming train of full and pressing days of work and labor and detail, of excitement and worry, of thoughtless spendthrift hours; we live from hand to mouth, we view life fragmentarily with no harmony of connectedness throughout the year. We view life like a child gazing through the play toy of a kaleidoscope, and we delight in the ever changing color scheme of the bits of painted glass within as we turn the thing around. And we think that is life! We consider our life from surface facts and never reach to the inner beauty and unity.

Never standing still in the way, never seeing beneath the painted surface of things, we come to have curious views of life; we see it either as a gay, brilliant soap bubble, coming from breath, filled with air and bursting into nothingness, *spurlos*, without a trace; or as a hideous nightmare peopled with the hag of want, with the witch of unreasoned fear, and with the specters of fate and destiny. The one view makes us shallow wantons, frittering away our few days of life with conscienceless thriftlessness, the other makes us arrant cowards and whimpering fainthearts afraid of our own shadows. Neither the one nor the other — wanton or coward — dons the crown of dignified manhood or the wreath of gentle womanhood; they neither hope nor aspire, they feel no thrill of great and stirring thoughts, they do not know the joy of coming near the high throne. They have been busy all the day, not standing in the ways, not standing still to consider the words of God. Like Caliban in Browning's searching poem, they either

... Sprawl, now that the
heat of day is best
Flat in the pit's much mire

or again like Caliban, they cower and hide when the
thunder and lightning come.

Stand in the ways and see — see beyond the surface,
beyond the material atoms and beyond chemical action,
beyond cells and protoplasm, beyond gravitation and heat
and light. These surely do not tell the whole story of
existence. What of love, admiration, service? What of sacrifice? Can gravitation explain any of them, do we find
an inkling of them in atom, protoplasm, cell? Can a thousand or a hundred thousand make in their aggregation
what we do not find in one cell — hopes, dreams and all
the glory of noble impulse, kindliness, brotherhood, and
charity? Stand in the way and see, instead of Haeckel's
blind, unreasoning, impartial forces circling us round
about and making our life a fearsome thing — stand and
see the Psalmist's conviction that "The Lord reigneth. He
is clothed in majesty." Stand still and consider the works
of God, and see, instead of a place of dread where the
inevitable and cruel decrees of Nature are worked out to
their bitter end, the assurance of the ancient singer: "The
Lord is mindful of His own." Stand in the ways and see
that instead of nothing but the laws of time and space
and matter we have also, as Pope asserts, vital sparks of
heavenly flame, not merely dull clods.

In this rushing world of ours, crowded with vast plans
for a new world, jammed with labor controversies, packed
tight with all that is explosive and disruptive — in this
world the men and nations who are not bent on individual
or national suicide must stop, stand in the ways and see.
They must find the way that is good, and find rest for
their souls in the kind of program of world peace which
will bring rest to the troubled myriads of humanity, not

for ten years, not for a generation, but as permanent a peace as is humanly possible. If the wise nations will but stop and see, they will be convinced that the world association of nations must be fashioned and put into effect within this year — if this jockeying for spheres of influence and balance of power is to be stopped before it wrecks the whole plan. *Rest for the world soul* — that must be the aim as we stop and consider the works of God.

Stop and see — consider the works of God — not obsessed with the wonder of towering skyscrapers, vast engineering schemes, Culebra Cuts, Muscle Shoals, T.V.A., Bonneville Dam Project, or Coolidge Dam; not blinded by the brilliance of the thousand inventions of these modern days. Stop and consider the *works of the Lord,* instead of these works of man which have brought no rest to our souls. What is the use of all these things of our vaunted twentieth-century civilization without the true joy of living, without happiness, without brotherhood, without faith in God, without plain honesty and simple honor? What is the use of this boasted modern progress without God? Of what worth is this monstrous, strenuous travail without the benefit of a guiding star? How low an age can sink when it denies or fails to note the height and lofty stature of the Godhead! If we but stand still — in the midst of these whirling days — and if we stop to consider, seeing the plan and the way of God, a new age may be rising out of this saddened and disillusioned half-century, the dawn of a wondrous day. Let us look forward, all of us! And may we help to usher in

> A thrilling age! A willing age!
> When steel and stone, when rail and rod
> Become the avenues of God,
> A trump to shout His thunders through,
> To crown the work that man may do.

IS SCIENCE ENOUGH?

But it is a spirit in man, And the breath of the Almighty, that giveth them understanding.
Job 32:8.

The spirit of man is the lamp of the Lord, searching all the inward parts.
Prov. 20:27.

I N A CITY of Ohio at the Red Cross Chapter House, the late Orville Wright and I were looking at a startling newspaper headline which told of a terrible battle in the clouds between hostile airplanes. It was early in 1918 and the battling planes were manned by German and American pilot aces. Mr. Wright, as you know, is the coinventor with his brother, Wilbur, of the first plane that really flew. For some time he was silent — and sad. Then he said to me, and I can remember the tone and almost the exact words to this day, thirty years after the conversation, "You remember Bobby Burns' lines, 'The best laid schemes o' mice and men gang aft agley.' We thought that our invention of the heavier-than-air flying machine would advance man's happiness, but it has become the swift messenger of death"... and then, after a rather lengthy pause, he remarked, "I fear we gave this to mankind before we were ready to control its use for blessing rather than for a curse; our spiritual and religious development has lagged behind the fast pace of science — hence this death from the skies!"

Orville Wright was the last man to champion the cause of science against the claims of religion, for he and his brother and sister were brought up in the devout and truly spiritual home of a bishop of the church. He was

December 12, 1948.

stating a fact in deepest sorrow — the lagging of the forces of the spirit; the sputtering of the candle of the Lord while the fierce bright light of science shone across the whole world. Certainly it is not intended in this discussion to pit science against religion or vice versa. They are not or should not be, in any sense, hostile to each other — they are different phases of God's self-revelation to His children.

There was a time, and many of us recall it with shame, when the representatives of the religious forces held science in utter opposition to religion and did so not only in debate, but actively in persecution. There is the rather depressing story of Galileo who was a scientist of note as well as the discoverer of a species of thermometer, a proportional compass or sector, and, most important, the constructor of the refracting telescope for his astronomical observations. In the course of his studies of the heavenly bodies he was convinced of the truth of the Copernican system that earth and planets move around the sun — and that the earth is not the center of the solar system. He was denounced as a purveyor of heretical teachings and, after a wearisome trial by the Inquisition, his judges condemned him to abjure by oath on his knees his scientific creed. This he did, but it is said that he whispered the words, *E pur si muove*, nevertheless it (the earth) does move. Some historians say that he was put to torture to make him abjure, though this is in dispute, while it is certain that he was threatened with it. He was sentenced, aged man that he was, to an indefinite term of imprisonment by the Inquisition. And he was only one of the scientists who met serious opposition from the forces of organized religion. That time of conflict between science and religion is, thank God, long past — and science has advanced with breathless speed during the nineteenth and twentieth centuries.

112

Science can speak for itself of the wonders which it has wrought. Scorning miracles, it has achieved many well-nigh miraculous things. It has ferreted out the forces and powers of nature and has in many cases harnessed them to perform much of the labor which was until recently done by human hands. It has leveled mountains and uplifted valleys, it has contained roaring and flooding rivers within the shores which it imposed. It has fought and conquered many of the diseases which have afflicted the human race, it has brought the refulgent light of electricity into our homes and streets and has connected us by wire — and then even without that wire — with the uttermost parts of the earth. It is now intently listening to the whisperings of the atoms and the neutrons — which the eye cannot see even when great magnification is applied. It has opened the era of atomic energy, with all the wonders that will be. But just as the airplane which the Wrights brought to us for blessing became a terrible messenger of death in war, so these new gifts of science may bring ever greater peril to mankind, and the atomic age may be the death knell of civilization and even of humankind on this earth . . . if we do not mend our ways.

Is science enough? That certainly is the important question. Was not that genial inventor who spoke to me in the Red Cross Chapter House in an Ohio city in 1918 right when he said that the corrective and directive which science needs is lagging far behind, that the terrific power which science put into our hands came before the human controls were ready? It is truly "the spirit of the Lord which giveth understanding; the candle of the Lord in the spirit of men searcheth all the inward parts!" We can command the lightning, as it were, but we have neither the wisdom, the understanding, nor the spiritual insight and the self-control and vision which religion provides to know what to do with it and where to direct it and when to withhold it from striking at our fellow-men. We have a very arsenal of power at our fingertips, but we have not learned how to use the steering wheel, and when to put our foot hard on the brakes. And hence the tragic situation in which the world finds itself, just three years after the last debacle of blind power uncontrolled, running riot without checkrein of any kind and without benefit of the sobering sense of morals, ethics, or spiritual values.

But there are those who will say, "That is the age-old, time-worn plea of the men of the Bible days, grown stale through the centuries, unheeded as the ringing of church bells, the call to worship and the chanting of litanies out of frayed prayer books and psalters." Yes, it is all too true, sadly true, that to many sophisticates, intoxicated with their mass of undigested facts from the outer fringe of science, and to those other men and women who have never cast off the Caliban insensibility, the spiritual call to the life of the spirit, to the vision upward toward life as God meant it to be, falls on utterly deaf ears as they rush headlong to their mess of pottage. So, for their sake, we turn to the only authorities whom they recognize and to whom at times they give heed.

What, for instance, does Louis Fisher, who has come close to the men who are making what the world calls "history," say? In a recent book, *Gandhi and Stalin*, Mr. Fisher compares these two world personalities with all their sharply contrasting and contradicting thoughts, motivations, and actions, one entirely depending on sheer brute power and the other on the spiritual forces which have held such an irresistible sway over masses of men through the ages. He shows these modern men — Stalin and Gandhi — each a type of those forces which are today in head-on collision, and he comes to the conclusion that "The crisis of our era is essentially moral," meaning thereby that only if the moral, the spiritual, and the religious point of view win out against immoral brute force is there a chance for human survival in this atomic age. The crisis is essentially moral — let us not forget it, let not the diplomats forget it, let us in our private and public life not forget it.

And after the writer and world correspondent, to whom India and Russia, Germany and England and the United States are but way stations in his perennial tours of the discovery of human motives and plans, I turn to the men who sit and work in the studies and the laboratories, to the scientists who do not dogmatize from half-baked knowledge. I have been reading, very slowly because the reading is hard and the thought tightly packed, the book by the scientist, Lecomte du Nouy, published early last year, with the rather staggering title *Human Destiny*. The author, who recently died, stood high among the internationally known French scientists and was at one time a co-worker with Dr. Alexis Carrel. In *Human Destiny* he seeks to reinterpret the theory of evolution in the light of modern physics, and he argues that the strictly materialistic theory of the universe and of man is no longer tenable. Man, he says, is not on this earth by chance alone. He contends that science finds a purpose, evident in the history of life, which rises above the laws of matter. According to his thesis, presented in his book with enormous erudition and the most advanced scientific learning, man has now, to all intents and purposes, completed his biological evolution and is just beginning his moral evolution. He sees in all life, as studied in the data of human history and in the test tubes of his laboratory, a divine purpose which rises above the laws of matter. A *divine purpose* — and hence a divine and spiritually attainable goal! So speaks a great scientist about human destiny.

And then I bring you the testimony of another scientist,

Edmund W. Sinnot, Director of Yale's Sheffield School of Science. The nation's top scientists gathered some time ago at Yale to honor the nation's first scientific research center, and one of its best, on the occasion of the centennial of the Sheffield School of Science. The director did not indulge in self-congratulation. "Science," said he to the assembly of scientists,

is modern, popular and dominant. It needs no special pleaders. It cannot be tempted to a certain arrogance and a conviction that the keys of truth are in its hands alone. . . . Logic and reason are no monopoly of science. To many thoughtful minds the gains of science are secondary and superficial things. Let us face the fact that what the world must have is a fuller cultivation of those qualities which are best termed spiritual. . . . Man leads a double life, of mind and spirit. . . . If spirit is suspect, as today when scientific materialism carries such authority, he is in danger of degenerating into a selfish and soulless mechanism. To be a whole man, he must cultivate both mind and spirit.

Thus spoke the head of Yale's Sheffield School of Science and also president-elect of the American Association for the Advancement of Science.

Clearly science is not enough; man is not only an exquisitely constructed physico-chemical mechanism but also a human being who has a soul to be saved or lost. He is not only a puny wick to be quickly burned out, but an immortal "candle of the Lord" to shine ever brightly on through eternity. We do not believe that "God has placed man upon the earth, bestowed upon him a mind to seek truth, a heart to perceive love and beauty," only to abandon us to the eternal midnight of the tomb. "Our life is more than a watch in the night"—"dust we are and unto dust we return, but the spirit born of God's spirit, breathed into the clay to animate and to ennoble, returns to God, the fountainhead of all spirits." These are the very words of our prayer book, full of the assurance of spiritual values, and without them our whole life would be empty and futile. Science is great, but it is not enough, as the great scientists themselves have insisted. With materialism rampant today, with national hates and greeds rising to a new crest, with psychopathic malaise and nervous breakdowns strewing our modern life-ways, the imperative need at this time is the cultivation of our spiritual forces, which may yet save us from another destructive war; there must be recognition of morals — the flowering of all true religion — in the conduct of our private and public living, and it may yet be that we shall thus achieve the serenity and joy and fulness of life's satisfactions which come through faith — through the healing waters which flow from the stream of organized religion, through public prayer and praise, through the salutary exercise of the powers of both mind and soul. Then will humanity again discover that the spirit of the Lord giveth understanding; that the candle of the Lord, searching our inward parts, will bring back the divine light into the dark and dismal places of our troubled modern lives.

THE HARDENED HEART
OR THE SERENE SOUL—WHICH?

Go in unto Pharaoh; for I have hardened his heart.
                                                    EXOD. 10:1.

Yea, the sparrow hath found a house, and the swallow
a nest for herself, Where she may lay her young;
Thine altars, O Lord of hosts, my King, and my God
— Happy are they that dwell in Thy house.
                                                    Ps. 84:4, 5.

I PRESENT here two contrasting texts — and set them side by side that they may more easily and obviously teach their lesson. The first text is from that chapter in Exodus, chapter 10, which treats of the time before the liberation of the Jewish people from Egyptian slavery. It is a strange text and has perplexed many people, even many casual readers of the Bible. It suggests that God predisposed Pharaoh, king of Egypt, to turn a deaf ear to the plea of Moses that he let his people free — and then punished him for the hardened heart. Is it possible that God should harden a person's heart and then punish him for the issues of that hardened heart? The verse needs explanation and interpretation.

God expresses Himself, realizes Himself in man and in nature through *Law* — Law whose immutability is its supreme worth. The order of the stars in their courses, the unvarying procession of the seasons, the unfailing transmutation of seed and soil and sunlight and rain into nourishing food — these are all beneficent because unvarying . . . God revealing Himself through Law — as in nature,

January 26, 1947.

118

so in the body and the mind and soul of man. Man, in harmony with God's law in his actions as well as in his thoughts, attains certain God-planned ends . . . his evil thoughts and actions come home to roost. So we interpret the Biblical text, "I have hardened Pharaoh's heart," to mean that God's law necessarily brought the hardened heart to the king. All his thinking and his greed for the unpaid labor of others — all his fears that the pulsating heart of freedom within the breast of the slave upon whom his foot rested would mayhap one day rise up in furious and devastating rebellion — all these things which were the natural outcroppings of his enslavement of a people caused his heart to harden, and inevitably brought him to the Red Sea of his destruction. His lust for power, his rigor of pride, and the driving torment of fear fixed him, mind and heart, into a set and stiff mold — hardened him, destroyed his peace, and inevitably pushed him to the fatal abyss.

This same operation of God's laws we see all about us; the same causes by which Pharaoh was hardened bring on the same loss of the sense of justice, the same violent grasp for power, and the same sickening fears which rob us of the enjoyment of life. Hence there arose at different times and in different parts of the world philosophies and disciplines which sought to soften the heart, to free the soul of those things that rob a man of his peace of mind. Came the Buddhist and taught that the peace of the soul can be attained only if we concentrate for long periods upon one, single, unchanging thought . . . a discipline of abstraction from realities . . . a removal of the mind, if one cannot remove the body, from the seething rush of daily life . . . peace by abstraction. Other philosophies induced religious groups to put themselves under a discipline which enabled them to separate themselves from the buffetings of our daily existence in some monastery or nunnery, or

119

in some ivory tower of their own fashioning, secluding themselves from the rough, tough storms which rage on lower levels. They sought peace by immuring themselves physically from life. And finally there are others — and their name is legion — who in their search for serenity, for happiness, immerse themselves completely in the details of business, profession, or pleasure hoping that thereby they may escape the multitudinous fears that haunt us, the fear of life's accidents, or the fear of death. Thus immersed completely in the rushing stream of unthinking busy-ness in gainful occupations, they have sought to elude the bogeyman of worry and fear, but instead they have added another torment to all the others, the scar of our modern civilization, stomach ulcers.

Not by abstraction from life, not by seclusion from its realities in some ivory tower, not by immersion in the breathless round of unthinking pleasure-seeking can serenity be attained. How then? We must put that question to ourselves and to society at large in our time because the distraught spirits in this emotionally disturbing age of ours are tremendously and terrifyingly on the increase. I do not speak of that tragic, increasingly numerous section of our society which fills our state hospitals — that is a problem by itself and we have hardly even sensed it, not to say tackled it. I am thinking of the millions who are in a constant fever of self-depreciation, who never are quite in harmony with their relation to life, never in a relaxed state, their whole being fluttering in a condition of imbalance; I am referring to that vast multitude who are beyond peace, beyond calm, beyond serenity.

To be sure, for some of them who have reached the serious stage of neurosis it is well to suggest the aid of dynamic psychology, some form of psychiatry. But most of these harried souls — and each one of us at one time or

another belongs to that category — can well find peace of
mind and serenity of spirit where it has been found in
all ages. The Psalmist offers it to us in the 84th Psalm:
"Yea, the sparrow hath found a house, and the swallow
a nest for herself where she may lay her young" — that is
their nature, there they are serene — but what have we,
the children of men? "Thine altars, my King, and my
God." The altars of religion are the founts of peace. What
is it that disturbs us and robs us of our peace? Matthew
Arnold in his poem "Empedocles on Etna" suggests the
way to discover the enemies of our peace of mind:

> We would have inward peace,
> But will not look within.

Religion suggests that we look within — its discipline, its
liturgy, its ceremonials, all are fitted and planned for the
look within, and then toward the approach to "Thine
altars, my King, and my God."

Looking within, we discover that one of the enemies,
the destroyers of peace of mind, is the conscience which
God gave us and which we have abused, so that it "doth
make cowards of us all." God gave us that conscience to
warn us of our transgressions, to urge us to come to His
altars and to confess our sins, to assure us that God
understands and will forgive, "for He knows," as Emerson said, "that there is a crack in everything He has made."
Conscience was not intended by God to be our bogeyman, to keep us constantly in jitters of self-condemnation;
it was intended to bring up into the light of day whatever
of evil was in us, in our consciousness, or our subcon-
sciousness, so that through confession we would attain to
self-understanding instead of neurotic self-condemnation.
That neurotic conscience which robs so many of serenity
can be healed through religion, "Thine altars," as for
instance through the healing discipline of the Day of

121

Atonement. "Thine altars" will wring out of conscience the cure of confession, of atonement, and will bring to us the consolation of forgiveness, "*Solachti,* I have pardoned." Thus through spiritual and religious artistry we will sublimate our imperfections into something ennobling and lovely in the sight of God.

And looking within we will discover that another enemy of human serenity is self-depreciation. The inferiority complex haunts many of us and takes its toll of our joy in living and striving. We get exaggerated ideas of other people's ability and subject ourselves to morbid self-criticism and self-flagellation. This enemy will be put to rout once we approach "Thine altars" and learn that God has made us all, each with definite limitations, and that it is the wise way for each of us to recognize them as being normal and then to proceed to a self-renunciation, putting aside those things which are beyond us — realizing that each human being must practice similar self-renunciation along the line of his limitation. God wants us to love ourselves, for how unless we love ourselves can we obey His command to "love our neighbors as ourselves"? Children of God — there should be no place in our thought of ourselves as being cursed by the inferiority complex.

The last and most powerful foe of serenity in man is fear. There is of course the normal fear which is self-preserving in the face of the thousand perils which are part of our life in this world; the fear, say, of fire, or of pain. It pushes us away from the destructive forces all about us. But the trouble is that so many of us are obsessed by neurotic fears, such as those that arise from personal anxieties, making us hypochondriacs, afraid of our health, worrying about this or that in our physical being which through our fear develops from a harmless condition into something baleful. Or we are afraid of some rift in our personality, lacking self-confidence, troubled by a feeling of insecurity, fearing the coming of failure into our life, imagining that we are objects of scorn or disapproval on the part of those whose opinion we most value. The most haunting of all these fears are the economic fears. These fears come to us only when and because we are worshiping the wrong God, dancing around the Golden Calf, which creates in us and our loved ones the demand — the excessive demand — for houses, for jewels, to be richer and have a finer house than our friends.

Thine altars — when we approach them in devout service to God a certain modesty in our drive for "things" takes hold of us, and a genuine contentment with our real contributions and achievements brings us spiritual healing. Thine altars, when we relearn the value of the things which finally count in life, will release us from the captivity of our fears of economic failure and the consequent tearing and debilitating worry. Nor must we submit to the metaphysical fear which haunts sensitive human beings who are afraid of death and oblivion. Of course we must recognize the brevity of human life here on earth and find wisdom through such contemplation. But surely our religion, whether Christian or Jewish, has taught us that we are firmly rooted in the Divine, and that therefore we need not fear our destiny here or in the world to come. "My times are in Thy hands" is the healing word of religion assuring us that we can never travel beyond the Everlasting Arms. Then indeed, when we lose a beloved one, we will escape the havoc to our serenity which assails those who sit hugging their grief unconsoled to their breast. As we approach "Thine altars," grief's slow wisdom will ripen within us and the words of faith will console us: "Thou wilt show us the path of life, in Thy presence is fullness of joy."

123

So the fears vanish, so at "Thine altars" we divest ourselves of morbid self-flagellation, of the inferiority complex and enslaving force of worry, adjusting ourselves through the ministry of religion to God and His world and to the limitations of our own life-force — and all perturbation will vanish. Thinking deep on the assuring promise of God which He spoke through the prophet Isaiah in chapter 54, verse 10, we shall when perturbed in spirit regain our serenity. Let us repeat the words over and over — thus:

For the mountains may depart, and the hills be removed; but My kindness shall not depart from thee, neither shall My covenant of peace be removed, saith the Lord that hath compassion on thee.

With this assurance, God's covenant of peace will be upon us — and we shall possess that peace of mind which we all seek.

WHERE IS THY GOD?

As OFTEN as we read through the Psalter, we are amazed to discover that there is no situation and no emotion in human life which has not been apprehended and faced and given literary expression in striking imagery or poignant petition. Psalmody is the thousand-stringed harp which brings forth the voice of the human heart in all its varied intonations. It cries out from the depths, it lifts our eyes unto the hills whence comes our help, it sings the paean of thanksgiving, and it intones the full-throated hymn of faith and trust when enemies rise up against us.

In all this psalmistry of the soul, there is one motif that seems to have been evoked especially for the benefit of our day and time. I refer to that poem of transcendent faith and hope, the 42nd Psalm. Let us briefly describe it; or rather let us examine the 42nd and 43rd Psalms, for they show a poetic unity of thought and treatment and were originally one, consisting of three strophes bound together by the same refrain. This Psalm begins with the thirst of the human soul for God, the living God, and tells how the Psalmist's soul pants after God as the hind panteth after running waters, ending with the phrase repeated at the end of each strophe, "The salvation of my countenance, and my God."

But this faith is not a facile and easily attained trust in a God who is obvious in all of life; it is a faith that strikes through a hard terrain of trouble like a glowing flower coming up amid rocks. The Psalmist who wrote this Psalm had worked his way up to God through a

November 3, 1940.

whole sea of doubt and despair, for he says, "My tears
have been my food day and night. ... As with a crushing
in my bones, mine adversaries taunt me; while they say
unto me all the day: 'Where is thy God?'" Out of that
abyss of sorrow and grief the poet passes on to the assurance that God is his salvation, that the hard-pressed soul
will yet sing to God a song of thanksgiving, that God will
champion his cause against an inhuman race and deliver
him from an unjust and treacherous people. And in the
end he bursts forth into a fervent prayer that is more
confidence than petition, "O send out Thy light and Thy
truth; let them lead me; Let them bring me unto Thy
holy mountain, and to Thy dwelling-places; Then will I
go unto the altar of God, unto God, my exceeding joy."
And then he ends with that sublime faith so sorely needed
by us today, "Why art thou cast down, O my soul? And
why moanest thou within me? Hope thou in God; for I
shall yet praise Him, The salvation of my countenance,
and my God."

The author of that song lived during the Babylonian
exile, some 2,500 years ago. But might he not as well be
a contemporary of ours, threatened by the same break-
down of humaneness, menaced by the same enemies, and
oppressed by the natural doubt and despair which follow
on the heels of moral degeneration in the world? See how
all the circumstances of this year 1940 fit with those that
faced the Psalmist 2,500 years ago in Babylonia. Note how
in our day there are millions who out of their misery can
ask, "When shall I come and appear before God?" Will
you not be able easily to discover the many who can well
exclaim, "My tears have been my food day and night"?
Think back the last year and a half, think of those Jews in
Central Europe shuttled between Germany and Poland,
neither wanting them, and now ravaged by a savage war
and its terrible consequences, think of those mothers and

babes, driven out of Sudetenland, living beneath the hedges and starving miserably; think of the suffering millions in all the conquered lands. Could not these millions in Germany, in Austria — that was — in Poland now again partitioned, and in the other countries which feel the heel of the conqueror, cry, "They crush me, body and soul"? Could they not honestly maintain that not only do they inflict these bodily wounds upon me, but also that these "mine adversaries taunt me"? They crush my bones — and not satisfied they besmirch my name among the nations. Shall I call the roll of the nations who lie crushed beneath the totalitarian juggernaut? We know them all too well and pity them. All of them cry out — "Where is thy God?"

Thus overwhelmed by the "waves and billows," few there are who would still proclaim, "Thou art the God of my strength!" Many of them would cry out as their soul sinks into despair what their tormentors use as a jibe: "Where is thy God?" Belabored and battered, scorned and scarred, is it any wonder that so many people are weighed down with doubt and despair? Take the case of Israel. Almost one half of the Jews of the world are cast into a veritable hell of hate while the other half are smeared with propaganda of racial inferiority, contemned and suspected as perfidious plotters against the weal of the world, in some lands stricken as we have not been since the Middle Ages. Is it any wonder that many of the victims of all this resurgence of the bestial and brutal begin to doubt that there is any moral order regnant in the world, and in despair cry out "Where is God?" With war again raging and dictators still malevolent and seemingly triumphant, it is natural to ask: "Where is thy God?"

These mockers and doubters are answered by the poet of the 42nd and 43rd Psalm — answered by the burst of faith, that God will "plead my cause against an ungodly nation," and "deliver me from the deceitful and unjust man." "Why art thou cast down, O my soul, and why moanest thou within me? Hope thou in God; for I shall yet praise Him, the salvation of my countenance, and my God." He will "send out His light and truth" to lead me.

But some there are who are so bereft of hope and faith that they would smile – if indeed in their misery and despair they could smile – at what they would call the naïveté of the Psalmist. For them I have other answers. Where is thy God? you ask. Is he dead – or is all the report of His existence a lie? Well, life isn't as simple as a straight line; God's world advances in no unbroken path, ever upward-moving. The march is like a spiral ascent, up, then down and backward, only to start upward on a higher level. The descent and the deterioration are there – have been there often in history, when men's dreams seemed to vanish, and when their finer spirit failed them. Those were dark ages. But as if the souls were renewed and refreshed by the spiritual slump, another age appeared that saw another and a further advance of humanity. The army of humanity retreats while it gets organized and poised for another ascent. Look at the story of the Jewish people. There must have been many who in doubt and despair cried out in the darkness of Egyptian slavery, "Where is thy God?" But God was there all the time – and He sent Moses. When Goliath mocked and raged and said "Where is your God?" that mocked God sent David and his slingshot. When Israel was taken into Babylonian exile there were the many who cried all the day, "Where is thy God?" In his own good time God sent Cyrus, the deliverer. God sends His messengers when the world is ready to give ear to the message. God is always here when the human channel is cleared for God's word.

There is another answer to your cry of despair – you who are troubled with the hate and inhumanity, the deterioration of moral stamina, the disregard of national obligations, the ineptness of statesmen who try appeasement and sacrifice nations that trust them, the selfishness of nations who deliberately bargain with dictators and sell their allies, and take home as an excuse for their perfidy the mean little trinket inscribed with the phrase, "Peace for our time" — only we now know that that trinket is discovered to be not only mean, but shoddy and phony, with no assurance of peace whatever.

To you who have seen all this and lost faith, I give you this answer. It is along two lines and asks these pointed questions: "Where is *your* God? and "*What* is your God?" As long as the God of mankind is Mammon, the living God cannot appear. So long as your God is of that pantheon where the human passions are deified, so long as many people worship the God of hate and cruelty and inhumanity, so long will there be a heavy drag on the wheels of man's progress, and so long will the living God fail to appear. It is the mass of humanity kneeling to the false gods which impedes the coming of God, the Father. To those who mock the victims of oppression and cruelty by jeering, "Where is thy God?" and to those victims who in their despair repeat the same cry, I give this challenge: "What is thy God?" In other words, it is not God who absents Himself from human affairs, but you who have shut Him out.

And again to those who say all the day long, "Where is thy God," I reply by a counter-question, "Where is *your* God?" Here is where this generation has been so noticeably and flagrantly derelict. Where is *your* God? Many there are who have relegated their God to His house, the church, the cathedral, or the temple. We come on the Sabbath and worship Him there, if we come at all, but forget Him the rest of the week in our daily lives. He stands eliminated definitely from our homes. He is not

129

remembered in prayers or in meditation. Our lives and our homes have become largely secular, and even paganized, and there is no room found for God. And then others there are who would in all honesty have to answer the question, "Where is *your* God?" by saying that they have entirely discarded Him, that He has no influence whatever in their lives. Perhaps they will say that they are getting on quite well without Him. There are quite a number of people who, though some do not quite admit it, have pushed God forcibly and entirely out of their living. They should be the *last* to cry out when the godless horde threatens them, "Where is thy God?"

And again there are those who would be forced to answer the counter-question, "Where is *your* God?" by admitting that mostly their God-recognition is lip service, with the self, the ego, pure and simple, excluding God and all else, a hypocrisy that bends the knee at the altar of God while the heart and mind are far away. What can you expect after such dereliction? And now we have a world where, as one keen observer has it, "everywhere everything seems rotten, silly and mad, little decency or hope or honor left, or any glory. Everywhere men fighting only for themselves, for their side, greedy, selfish, not caring what happened to anybody else. It's the fashion now — with this new cult of lip service that reduces God to a thoughtless nod of faint recognition — to laugh, to roar, to hoot and make wisecracks about the things for which men died."

No, the fault is not God's now that the nations rage — He is not absent from His world. We do not let Him in. That war and dictators, cruelty, hate, and godlessness may cease, let us bring Him in with the prayer, "Send out Thy light and Thy truth; let them lead us; let them bring us unto Thy holy mountain, and to Thy dwelling-places, that we may go unto the altar of God, unto God,

our exceeding joy." Then indeed, in His own time, our
God will be our salvation.

THE VOICE OF GOD IS CALLING

THE GREATEST of theophanies is majestically introduced by the phrase, "And the Lord came down upon Mount Sinai, to the top of the mount" (Exod. 19:20). And then we read how the crashing thunder and the flaming lightning formed Nature's appropriate accompaniment to the divine revelation of the Ten Commandments on Mount Sinai. So awe-inspiring is the coming of God to these men and women just out of Egypt that they ask their leader Moses that he should speak to them and not God, lest they die. Alone comparable to the grandeur of this theophany, this appearance of God to men as described in the Scripture, is that set forth in the sixth chapter of Isaiah. Here the court of seraphim surrounding God sing "Holy, holy, holy," while one of them purifies with the live coal the lips of the young prophet who is destined to be the mouthpiece of God.

But though these stand out because of their grandeur and majesty, the Bible is full of theophanies. Almost on every page of certain large sections of the great book God reveals Himself to someone of His chosen ones, speaks His message, announces a doom or promises a great hope. Thus we read how Israel proceeded to build a tabernacle in response to God's command *"V'osu li-mikdosh v'shochanti b'sochom,"* "Let Israel build me a sanctuary and I will dwell in their midst." God was to dwell in the midst of His people, was to be their familiar. And to Solomon, who built the great Temple at Jerusalem, he says, "If you will walk according to my statutes and do

---

December 15, 1940.

my commands, then I will dwell in the midst of the children of Israel, and I will not forsake my people Israel." In all these instances the underlying thought that is present impressively is that God walks with men and lives amongst men and talks to men "face to face."

And it seems to me that thinking men and women cannot escape the series of questions that so easily obtrude themselves upon our twentieth-century consciousness. These are: Did God in reality reveal Himself to men on earth, at Sinai, at Jerusalem, at Bethel, to Moses, to Amos, to Hosea, to Isaiah, to Jeremiah, to all the rest of the great men who speak in the name of the Lord? If He did in reality reveal Himself, what was the manner of the revelation? And most important question of all, has God ceased His revelations to men, or are there Sinais now as then? Does God speak to men today?

The first question is largely a question of the veracity of the witnesses in the cases involved. Read casually through the Bible, open at almost any page and you will note the thousands of statements that God revealed Himself, that men were convinced that they had heard God's voice, that He had actually talked to them. You will realize, as you read, that these many witnesses did not use a figure of speech when they said that God spoke to them, but that they were sure that it was an actual auditory experience that had been theirs. Their ears heard the message that they were then told to deliver to the people, and they never questioned but that that message came directly, externally as the voice of God. How shall you treat these many witnesses?

A school of thought, fashionable in the latter half of the nineteenth century, with Robert Ingersoll as their apostle, laughed the pretensions, as they called them, of these witnesses out of court. To these men Moses was a trickster, with the very best of intentions, yet withal a trickster who took the occasion of a terrible thunder and lightning storm to palm off on a credulous people a code of commandments as having been spoken by God in the midst of the terrifying disturbances of nature. To them the lawgiver was a benevolent sleight-of-hand man, a magician learned in the ways of deception. To them the prophets were wise statesmen or religious enthusiasts who sought to give weight and authority to their self-appointed task by falsely insisting that they were but uttering the mandates of God who had spoken to them. Is that a correct appraisal of these men? Read again the story of Moses and see if it reads like the story of a trickster. Peruse again the flaming pages of the prophets, who gladly gave themselves to a possible and even to an actual martyrdom, who cast their reproaches in the face of the populace time and again, and judge, then, if they could stoop to a deception. And yet they said, "God spoke to me," and yet they insisted that their message was but the utterance forced from them by divine compulsion. The testimony of these unimpeachable witnesses has therefore generally been accepted that God did actually reveal Himself to men in the days of which the record speaks.

As to the manner of the revelation they did not say much that would help us to understand the process. We get very little insight there into how the Divine infiltrated into direct relation with the finite. There seems to have been so little question as to the possibility and the actuality of the revelation, that the manner and process of it was not dwelt upon. To them it was the content of the message of God, not the manner of its transference to men, that was important, for it was the content of the message that was called into question by their contemporaries, never the process. But while we do not know how God spoke to Moses and the prophets, we do know how they prepared themselves for the message, we do discover

certain operations and dispositions in the life of the
prophet which seemed to wear thin the partition that
divided him from the Divine. There were training schools
for the prophets which gave a man what a school could
toward the development of disposition, the accumulation
of information, and the focusing of thought upon the
possibility of such communication from the Divine. There
was an atmosphere of holiness and solemn devotion and
fervent expectancy in these schools, so that the royal
Saul, who came to such a school with murder in his
heart, was so tremendously influenced by the holy spirit
of the place that he remained to pray.

It seems, too, that one of the positive prerequisites was
the surrendering of the prophetic mind to long periods
of meditation, with an inexorable call to go out of the
clamor of the city into God's silent places. Moses went
into the wilderness and gave himself to years of earnest
meditation. Out of the silences God came to him, out of
the great reaches of space the voice of God called him to
his mission. It was thus in the calm of the wilderness,
away from the haunts of men, that they wooed God to
their souls. It was through this trinity of disciplines that
the tympanum, which with the rest of the mortal beings
held God off from the consciousness of men, became thin
and sensitive enough to vibrate and thus transmit the
message of God to the select on earth. It was to those
who submitted to this discipline that the word of God
came and with it an unfailing conviction that God in very
fact spoke the message. And with that assurance they
confidently gave what was a novel and oft unwelcome
pronouncement to men.

But the important question it seems is: Does God speak
to men now? Surely if God in the olden days spoke to
men, He did not suddenly remove Himself from the
haunts of men; He did not at a certain period in the

history of the race – say at about the beginning of this era, 2,000 years ago – permanently build up a wall between Himself and His children. Surely the promise uttered through the Psalmist: "If with all your hearts ye seek Me, ye shall find Me," holds good with us as with those of an earlier time. Why do we, most of us, not hear God? Is not this the reason: that we do not seek Him, either with whole heart or even with half a heart? At the very outset we do not find God because we have no expectation of finding Him. All our training is against it. We live in a scientific and materialist age. We deal with matter, with the tangibles, with atoms and ions, which by the force of gravitation and a few other similar forces have not only made the world we live in, but have fashioned us who live in the world. In the scheme of life as thus developed where can God come in? Where can there be any expectancy of God? To be sure, that sorry scheme of life doesn't explain one-tenth of life. It doesn't explain the thrill of high resolve, it doesn't explain love, it doesn't explain sacrifice – the sacrifice for a flag, a cause, an idea. How can the whirl of atoms explain the answer of the frail soldier-son of Professor Foster of Chicago University, who died of pneumonia in a southern camp during the first World War? When his father asked him, in 1917, if he should use his influence to have him exempted because of his natural frailty, he answered: "I have no more right to live than others." But thus by gravitation, molecules, atoms, ions, and gases, we have tried to explain all of life: thus we have been taught in the schools for a hundred years. How can we see God, how hear Him when our entire training has found no place for Him? Not expecting, we do not note.

And then the atmosphere of these generations has very little that would prepare us to hear God. It is the crude air of the market place, it is the evaluation of life as by a ledger and through the spectacles of a bookkeeper. The smoke of the chimneys of industry blinds us to the daily revelation of God; the whirl of the wheels drowns out the sound of God's voice. The chatter of the market place has superseded high converse and solemn meditation. We do not go out into the quiet places, out into the wilderness, to habituate the eye to bigger and wider horizons and to attune the ear to the weighty message. And today it is worse, for we have added to the noise of industry the clatter of the machine gun and the shriek of the bombs from the air. But God is still in His world and He still speaks to us.

What was the World War but the registry of God's presence with us? The nations of the earth and the individuals of which these nations are composed had gone their way frowardly, the way of Babylon and Rome. Lust and greed and injustice held sway as in the worst days of Nero. Men were getting hardened by ease. This cataclysmic sorrow hurried across the heart of humanity as the very hand of God that it might bring us to a halt in our headlong rush to perdition: that it might soften the stony-hearted; that it might stir to thought the thoughtless; that again we might have the long-vanished enthusiasms for justice and honor, for right and truth. All this we had to learn by drinking the bitter hemlock-cup of war's hard tribute. So God spoke in other days. And when the war failed to make men and nations listen to God's voice, the depression came. And, as that did not suffice, came this second tragic world war. Might He not be speaking today? Today in the world's history more than in any other time? Was there ever a more riven, confused and perplexed and sick world? Did mankind ever need light and guidance as much as now? The world waits for the voice. And what hear we? The piping of little wits, the trivialities of dilettantes, the roaring of empty-headed and coarse demagogues. What does God say? All we hear is what Lenin and Trotsky said and what Stalin says today — what Hitler and Mussolini orate; not an eternal and lasting truth, but the little partial truths and the great, impertinent lies to tide them over today and perhaps tomorrow.

Europe is filled with hate and greed and murder. Surely God is speaking, entreating, appealing. Yet all we hear — or give our ears to — is the wrangling of politicians and their haggling for territorial additions, Transylvania or the Dobruja. Our ears are deafened by Hitler's insane shrieking and Mussolini's boasting and Laval's rationalizing of his own treachery; each seeking, not the great equation that shall solve the problem of all Europe, but rather the little temporary advantage for his own country.

And as for America — our country — are we hearing God's voice, have we submitted ourselves to the disciplines which would bring Him near us — are we seeking Him? In this crucial hour in the world's history do we not deserve the bitter reproach of Elijah at Carmel as he cried to his people, "Why halt ye between two opinions: If Baal is your God, serve him, but if the Lord is your God, serve Him!" God speaks — if only we might hear amid the awful din of destruction in these days:

> The voice of God is calling its summons unto men,
> As once He called at Zion, so now He calls again.
> Whom shall I send to succor my people in their need?
> Whom shall I send to shatter the bonds of lust and greed?

And from the great multitude that has so long been on its knees to trivial idols may there arise the glad shout:

> We hear, O Lord, Thy summons and answer here are we,
> Send us upon thine errand, let us Thy servants be.
> Take us and make us holy; teach us Thy will and way;
> Speak, and behold, we answer, "Command and we obey."

138

GOD SPOKE AMID THE TUMULT

OF THE WORLD

When it was morning, there were thunders and light-
nings and a thick cloud upon the mount and the voice
of a horn exceeding loud.... And God spoke all these
words.   Exod. 19:16; 20:1.

HUNDERS AND LIGHTNINGS and a thick cloud and
the sound of the trumpet, these are the phenomena with which a new generation is becoming
familiar even as the generation before it did, through
the first World War. Again is the world in tumult —
thunders of guns and cannon in China, in Russia, in the
Solomons, and in North Africa make an ever increasing din. The lightnings of incendiary bombs strike ships
and stately public buildings and peaceful homes and snuff
out many lives. The thick cloud of hate and distrust,
international, interreligious, interracial, darkens the face
of the earth. And through it all is heard the strident
trumpet sound of war's alarms. If at any time the next
procedure mentioned in our text was needed it is this
fifth decade of the twentieth century. After the thunder
and the lightning and the thick cloud, there followed
the spoken word of God. "And God spoke these words."
Now, now, as seldom before, we need the speaking voice
of God. At that time to which our text refers God's voice
gave His people the revelation of the Ten Commandments, the heart and center of the moral law. And it is
something just as impressive in the moral sphere that we
need today. We see the taking of God's name in vain, non-

November 22, 1942.

observance of God's holy days, irreverence to parents, disregard of the sanctity of the home, murder, theft, and greed, not only in the life of individuals but on the national and international scale. The Nazis have removed the landmarks, so have the Fascists and the Japanese. "And God spoke." There are three ways of facing a world at war. One is to let "the tumult of the world grow dull upon our inattentive ear," the while we note how

> The evening's blessed stillness covers all
> And o'er the fields she folds her cloak of grey,
> And softly twilight falls and toil doth cease;
> While o'er our soul God spreads His mantle — Peace.

In other words, we can for the moment become tumult-deaf and violence-blind, and say "God's in His heaven, all's right with the world." This world of self-delusion is very pleasant; the only trouble is that the sad awakening soon comes and it is the harder and rougher and more cruel realization because of the pleasant dreams which delayed the waking hour.

A second way is one that many have perforce already adopted in these days as others did in similar periods of turmoil. It is exemplified by the peasant who continued to plow his farm while the shells of the crazed world exploded nearby, by the scientist who did not interrupt his experiments though the roof of his laboratory was demolished by gunfire, and by the Red Cross nurse who bandaged the wounded in the open fields just behind the lines in an active sector with the same unhurried movements as if she were in her old hospital of St. Luke's in New York. In the same way there are many people who just "carry on," drawing about them the charmed circle of those who are "serene with God." It sounds selfish, but it is just such souls who keep a maddened world a-going. Not many of us can adopt this course.

The third way is to look at this tumult of the nation in historical perspective and to see it as part of the gradual transformation of man from brute to barbarian, from barbarian to civilized being. History will reassure us that new eras with all their birth pangs mean higher levels of life. And our text teaches that thunders and lightnings and the voice of trumpets were the setting of the revelation of the Ten Commandments, that storm and stress always hang about our Sinais, that the emergence of man on higher levels shakes the very heart of the world. Tumult — and the still, small voice of God. Only if we hear that voice amid the tumult will the world find the basis of permanent security and peace. This last group who have the urge to still the tumult and bring order into the chaos so that at least our children may live in a civilized world, and that something of happiness may come — these to whom it is hoped many of us belong — ask themselves, how can the still small voice be heard, what may bring sanity, decency, honor, and peace back again?

What says the still small voice amid the tumult and the storm? Can happiness and the civilized life be attained through education alone? There are those who have thought that was the supreme message of the still, small voice. If only people could be educated — through the process offered by the schools — as they are at present or in the near future, they would be civilized. We have had much of this education and where are we? In Germany the educated, so-called, even the professor class and in general the faculties of the universities, stood silent while the learned books of non-Aryans as well as of men like Thomas Mann, the Aryan, were being burned, while their most respected colleagues were forced out of the faculties because they happened to be Jews or liberals. Above all they were silent while wisdom and science were mocked at with the promulgation of pseudo-scientific racial theories and eugenic hypotheses as the quintessence of the knowledge of the German universities. Many professors publicly espoused these unscientific race theories. Speaking by and large, the rape of the universities found the professors silent, in many cases acquiescent. Their education, vaunted as a redeeming process, had not made them either strong characters or courageous ones. And this silence stands out in impressive contrast to the vocal and heroic front of religion against a similar planned rape of the church. No, not education — education alone holds no salvation in its hands. A happier time can't come that way to the world. Alone, it is impotent.

But religion, at its best, can assuage the evil. The storm and tumult reveal three centers of this noisy and catastrophic eruption. It is to these that we must turn our attention, these that we must counteract — these that we must eliminate and render nugatory and ineffective; and this can be possible only through the efficacy of those convictions and predispositions which religion offers. The three storm centers that have brought on our modern tumult can easily be sensed. First, there is the popular realism that has brought a serious disintegration into our mental and emotional life. Every young person (that I know) who makes any pretense of thinking is trying hard to be realistic. He may be romantic or idealistic by the set of his nature, his temperament, but he tries hard not to let anyone know it. Realism is the word today, clear-eyed, unblinking recognition of life's stern and ugly facts, with no feeling of one's self. Pleasing sentimentality, wishful thinking, idealizations, comforting faiths, satisfying optimisms — these are the devils of the new generation. Nothing will do except realism.

Yes, let us be realistic. Healthy realism is a great asset. The writers of the Bible were realists. You will look in vain for a single area of life which the Bible does not see

142

clearly and about which it does not speak candidly. Let
us see all the ugly spots of life as realistically as does the
Bible, and then we may be moved to do something about
them. Above all, let the urge come to us to do something
about them. To be cynical about all this ugliness in life
and to do nothing about it — which is the attitude of so
many realists — is a sorry sort of philosophy. The true
realist sees the ugliness and cruelty of life and tries to
mitigate it. Nay more — the true realist does not say or
think that only ugly things are real, that sewers are the
only real things, but he notes that fresh purling mountain
streams are real too, and flowers and the sunrise. You
cynics, you whose thinking and living and novels note
only the base and the ugly, the trouble with you is not
your realism but your lack of it in its completeness. There
is a reality of beauty, of pity, of spiritual living, a reality
that outlasts the realities of ugliness and hate and cruelty.
It was the unreal realism, making sport of the idealism
of an earlier generation, which brought its crop of cynical
ruthlessness in politics, warfare, and the daily life. It said,
man is a brute. And as so often happens, many lived up
to that pronouncement; hence the tumult of the world.

And the second center is the selfishness that became
common and sought to become respectable through the
philosophy of egotism. It dethroned God and set up the
Ego, the self. It abolished all sanctions and said human
desire is the measure of right. It laughed the Ten Commandments out of court and set the law of insatiable self-
satisfaction above everything else. Of course, there was
some hypocritical piety which publicly gave lip service
to the Ten Commandments and other divine sanctions
and statutes, but in practice recognized nothing beyond
and above Self. And so greed and cruel exploitation entered on a new highroad toward what proved a disastrous
jumping off place, the abyss in which the world finds

itself today. Selfishness has been placed above social needs, greed for special privileges above our country's tragic and crying need, the Ego above God; hence the tumult.

And the third center of the storm is a vast force of hatred and fear and mistrust which has been loosed upon the world. We had thought that humanity had so far shed its bestiality that nothing like the sadism and race hatred now abroad in some lands could ever find room in the human heart. We have come to learn that there are still some very dark areas of human nature which need the illumination of human decency and trust and love.

Yes, dear friends, this half-realism of the sewer and the gutter, which makes people hard and cynical but not wise, this selfishness and greed which arise from the worship of the ego, this hatred and fear which crush out the embers of social justice and human decency and mercy — all these will be cast out of the human soul by the tumult that they have caused in the world. And it may well be that out of the noise and confusion, again as so often in history since Sinai, the still small voice will be heard above and after the thunders and the lightnings — and God and His Law, and righteousness and idealism and sanity and honor and decency, will have been proven the better and the wiser part. Out of pain come many blessings, out of the tumult of the world may come the outlines of a New Heaven and a New Earth. Let God speak! Let the still small voice of religion be heard! Let us help fashion that new world, and the days to come may yet hold for us, and for mankind, life and contentment and happiness.

FALSE GODS:

THE GOLDEN CALF AND OTHERS

THE CENTURIES as they come and go witness one eternal struggle, the fight against the false gods. At times it has seemed as though the false gods had so securely entrenched themselves that they were here to remain to the end of the story; but at others man seems to rise to new spiritual peaks of insight and power and then the *Goetterdaemmerung*, the twilight of the gods, appears imminent. Some of the false ancient deities have already gone down to oblivion — Horus and Osiris and Isis, once worshiped in stately ceremonial on the banks of the Nile; Ormuzd and Ahriman, once venerated by the Persian; Marduk of the Babylonians; Zeus, Dionysus, Bacchus, Venus and Adonis, Jupiter and Mars of the Greeks and Romans — all of these have gone to their twilight. Their day was: it is unrecoverable.

That information can be picked up in any average history of the world. But it is well for man to learn what somehow the histories do not always give, that every fallen false god is a symbol of man's spiritual ascent, is the very step upon which he rises to a higher level for a truer and more exact survey of his world. It was a very thoughtful philosopher who said, in all reverence I am sure, that man creates his God in his own image and likeness.

No matter how clearly God may have revealed himself to man in the Bible, that revelation is just so many words which must be interpreted and experienced by each human heart and soul; hence each individual creates his own god, like unto himself. The human features and emotions in the god, heightened immeasurably, are still discernible. Thus each individual, each age, each level of culture and civilization, creates its god, or rather interprets the divinity perceived by all in the universe, in those terms that that age and group can understand.

And it is therefore natural that as the age gets mellow and mature, as civilization advances and human culture heightens, the conception of God which was adequate and true to the earlier centuries becomes a false god who must be broken to pieces before man rises to higher levels. The recognition that there were and are false gods is but the proof of our spiritual progress and ascent.

False gods are not easily retired, largely because not all members of the human group have equal spiritual growth. Many peoples, groups, and individuals show symptoms of spiritual lag. Israel at Sinai was cognizant of a visible revelation of God, clothed in the majesty of the moral law, the Ten Words. And yet once the dominant personality of Moses, who took part in the process of revelation of God, was removed for a little while a large section of the people demanded a return of the old gods, among them the Golden Calf. No doubt those who danced around the idol in wild orgy were of that portion of the delivered people who were referred to in other parts of the wilderness story as "the mixed multitude." There was a large group at any rate, in Israel — as there is with every people — that lagged behind those to whom the revelation at Sinai was a vivid reality. The mixed multitude is everywhere holding back the progress of the world, in all spiritual aspects, sodden and without ideals, always lured and captivated by the near and the concrete; and this happens because of their arrested development, because of their defective mental vision, because the lofty thought and abstraction are unintelligible gibberish to them. The mixed multitude dancing around its false god, its molten image of the calf, had but a short hour of gay orgy; for soon the golden calf was unsettled from its pedestal and burned in the flames, and its ashes were placed upon the tongue of every one of its worshipers — the ashes of disappointment, sorrow, low ideals, and death.

The old story is as new as though it had happened the day before yesterday. The false gods are dead, but false gods are ever newly created. New false gods, or rather frequently old false gods in new guises, are raised on pedestals; men give their all for them, dance about them, and pay them homage, crying, "There are thy gods!" That is the perennial cry. The ways of the Puritan get tiresome to a certain unregenerate section of humanity; sitting with the glare of righteousness full upon them a crowd under some cave impulse forms and raises the cry for a golden calf, for something nearer to the brutish in man, something nearer to his own image, something with which he will feel at home. And then, as in the old story, follows the necessary sequel: the tables of the Ten Commandments, the moral law that kept us on a high and often uncomfortable Sinai, are broken.

Nowadays we haven't, to be sure, any golden calf as our false god, but by no means are we free from the sin of the mixed multitude. As long as man progresses — and hasn't quite achieved the goal of humanity, which will be as long as man lives — there will be false gods, the relics of a preceding generation's veneration which are still hugged close to the breast of the spiritual and mental laggards of the present age. These are thy gods!

How many still believe in a god of vengeance? It is a false god who takes his toll from his worshipers in making the world a terrific place of fierce judgments. The god of war, the lord of hosts, of armies, the god of battles, the god of favorite and chosen peoples — Semitic or Nordic, we care not which — are all false gods, which eventually must be burned, while their ashes come upon the tongues of the worshipers in sorrow and disappointment.

Great masses of humanity in this twentieth century are still dancing around those old false gods, which is but an indication that we have not made such tremendous progress in the spiritual life as the advance in material things would have led us to expect. Great masses of men are still back there in the wilderness, four thousand years back, dancing around their golden calf; others are anachronisms that belong in the dark ages, that are willing to howl down witches and burn them as possessed of the devil, that talk of the devil as though he were a very person dressed in red and to be distinguished from honest folks by a cloven foot.

But there are less obvious false gods whom many of us worship, for whom we are ready to give a great deal, money, health, and very life. Come forth, ye worshipers of the false god of luck, of fortune. I am especially referring to those foolish people who listen with bated breath to the astrologer about "their star," who will not sit down to a table with twelve other people "because it is bad luck," or who will not walk beneath a ladder for the same reason, or who speak of numerology as a new revelation, or who have a thousand and one strange symbolisms of good and bad luck, from a black cat crossing one's path to a lucky rabbit's foot or a lucky stone. How many there are who are thus superstitiously credulous — but who stoutly claim themselves skeptics in religion. However, these superstitions do not as a rule get deep down into the character of a person and change the current of his being and feeling and thinking life.

But unfortunately there are those who trace everything back to the god of fortune, of good or bad luck, those who get the conviction that there is no inherent virtue or worth to the man or woman who attains a measure of prosperity, but insist that it is all luck, just good fortune, thereby relieving themselves of all measure of blame for their own failures by saying that the fickle god of fortune failed to smile on their venture.

If we worship that god, as many do, the acrid ashes come upon our tongue; we lose all initiative and courage; our hands are tied while we wait for the god of luck to move; we become inert and leave all to the turn of fortune. This worship of the god of fortune is far more prevalent than we imagine. The gaming table is one of his many altars and here alone millions of his devotees crowd around and lose friends and health and time and whatever money they may possess.

Then, too, stand forth ye who bend the knee to the new god called material success, who if we scrutinize his features will be discovered to be just another golden calf, another god Mammon. Success that the world might acclaim us, success that is measured only in dollars and in power; how clearly it has become "the great god Buddha" of this age!

Anyone who fails to bend the knee to it is either called a fool, as the play of that name by Channing Pollock depicts, or is suspected of being a hypocrite. The worshipers of material success can't imagine anything else to grip the soul of any sensible human being as a life motive — neither love, nor honor, nor human service, for any of which three many a man and woman has bartered away success and discovered that he or she did not get the worst of the bargain by any means.

And look what men devote to the god success! If men were asked to give to the living God one-tenth, one-hundredth of what they gladly give to success, they would consider it the height of unreasonable demand, another symptom of hierarchical presumption. At any rate, they refuse to give it to the living God. But to material success they give all their days and their thoughts, their health and their strength, and alas, how frequently they give their most precious possession, their very soul.

And the third false god whom this age worships is the god Efficiency. We think that this humanity of ours is just a great machine, and if only the cogs fit aright, if only the pistons are oiled carefully and kept to the highest point of material efficiency, then all human ills will disappear. Political economy and industrial efficiency are the great deities of the machine age. Salvation through efficiency is the slogan. The law of supply and demand and the other economic laws are raised to the dignity of the Ten Commandments. We are beginning to forget, and in the totalitarian nations they have already forgotten, that man is not a machine at all, that he is a spiritual entity. Not that we should believe this world ought to be run in a slovenly and inefficient manner, but rather that we should be on guard against taking the heart out of business and industry, and eliminating kindliness from the most frequent relations of men. Efficiency will certainly not bring salvation. Efficiency experts do not consider as at all valuable the great assets of loyalty and love that men can throw into the stream of human endeavor, assets which in spite of the new vogue and the new false god are almost incalculably great in power.

Other false gods find their thousands of devotees offering incense unto them: the god of riotous living, really Dionysus of old, the god of greed, the god of the ego, of individualism whose priest and prophet was Ibsen and whose acolyte was Nietzsche. So rose the idea of the Superman — a new false god — who is a law to himself, proud of his strength; ruthless Superman worshiping himself the false god. How much we offer and sacrifice to these false gods! Hence this writhing world, hence these heartaches of the modern man. And therefore, too, are the tablets of the law broken, and the leaders of men sorrowful. These lesser gods must go! These Fuehrers and Duces and sacrosanct Emperors must be dethroned. The gold calf must be ground to the dust. The conception of the true God and an understanding of His will must reach the heart of men, of the mixed multitude, before democracy and brotherhood and human decency and kindliness can flower forth in fullest splendor upon this earth.

THE RELIGION OF THINKING MEN

THE POPE has called for a year of earnest religious thought. Why not dedicate this second Sunday of the planned year to thinking about the fundamentals of all religions? To this let us set ourselves.

During the past fifty years a sharp wind has been blowing through the peaceful vale of religion. Perhaps only three other times in history has there been such a stirring up, such a searching of hearts, such a breaking from the moorings as we witness during this period. The wind blew across the landscape of faith in the days of the prophets, and entrenched priesthood with its pomp of spectacle and sacrificial altar was loosened from its foundations and slowly slid out of existence. Again it blew across the field of faith, especially in the heathen world of the Roman Empire, at the opening of this era two thousand years ago, and a greater purification and more robust ethical life came into existence. The third time the cosmic tempest of the soul broke upon this earth was during the first half of the sixteenth century, and it produced the Protestant Reformation.

Again the wind blows in the region of the faiths. Authority in religion is not even the shadow of its former self. Tradition is a pale ghost for influence. "Thus said the fathers; so states the book," are as futile and vain to hold back the floods of questionings as was the command of King Canute to the waves of the ocean to roll no farther upon the shore. The waves continue to wash the sands of many religions, and they are carrying into the sea many a formerly treasured dogma or doctrine or ceremonial. People are not these days accepting things in the domain of religion without thought and questionings.

152

But we must not be misled by these very certain signs upon the horizon of the faiths into thinking that religion is failing. Religions are weakening, theologies are becoming ragged banners that no longer bring on the rallying of great groups, anemic and pale are the man-made creeds; but religion is stronger than ever before. It is more potent now than ever before, perhaps for the very reason that the fresh, purifying wind of inquiry has stirred through the valley of faith and has separated forever the living flesh from the dead bones, perhaps for the very reason that men are not accepting their religion, but each one of us is re-creating it for himself.

Religion is a deeper force in men's lives today because we are getting more and more disrespectful of labels. Labels are useful as articles for classification, rough and crude and undiscriminating as they are even in that limited field. But we have come to see that the label is not the thing. People did not see that some years ago. You were either respectable or not, righteous or not, saved or damned, depending upon the label that you bore. The label was the thing, then, both to the world here and to St. Peter or whoever else held the gate of paradise. Many persons were satisfied with the label and never tried to get at the nourishing contents of the labeled receptacle. Now people look at the label, but they use the sharp instrument that admits them into the contents. They are satisfied now only when they can sample the contents beyond the label. They are thinking in the matter of religion as in all other things. Men once thought themselves out of the divine right of kings; we are thinking ourselves out of the obsession of war into world peace; we shall also think ourselves into religion instead of into labels. It shall be not a thing on the outside, an appendage, but very close to us, "in thy heart," a very living, palpitating part of our very selves, the best of ourselves.

And the God of that religion is more than the "God of my fathers." He is "My God."

A decade or more ago a monarch, when asked what his religion was, said: "The religion of thinking men" — a very happy coinage. Is there anything definite and concrete in that phrase, or was it a mere subterfuge to hide behind? There are some who will abide by Herbert Spencer and his doctrine of the unknowable, and say that the religion of thinking men is agnosticism or no religion. But in answer I place beside Spencer that true thinker and philosopher, the lens grinder of Holland, the Jew, Spinoza, the philosopher's philosopher. That he was at least as much of an inveterate thinker as was the agnostic of the nineteenth century is witnessed to by Goethe, who says: "What especially riveted me to him was the boundless disinterestedness that shone forth in every sentence," his objectivity both in thought and in practice. And the result of Spinoza's thinking is found not in a vague unknown *amor intellectualis Dei*, but the emotional recognition of God. His religion was "cosmic emotion," a very different thing from the blank negation of Spencer.

The real thinker, the real philosopher, doesn't mechanically limit his researches to those fields that only admit the use of ratiocination. He knows that the very depths of things, the very heart of things must be plumbed by the intuition. He knows that the truest things are perceived by a faculty beyond reason, a great flame in the very depth of self. And that inner light of ours takes us beyond the field to which science introduces us, and makes us truly at home in our world.

Science makes us perceive the many, makes us learn all about the many, and find the various laws under which the many work; but the intuition makes us perceive the one in the many, and so directs us to find our way in the world labyrinth and makes us feel at home in the world.

154

Science perplexes us with the many and diverse things of the world, and going upon the assumption that the world is hostile, tries to learn its secrets in order that it may subdue and conquer it. Through our intuitions we see the one in the many, the one that explains it all. Instead of the burden of the universe, so oppressive, it reveals the heartening lure of the universe. Under its view the world, grand beyond compare, calls to us, beckons to us. So intuition does not stand opposed to the intellect, and the result of intuition or religion does not stand antagonistic to science; they are complementary to each other. They view different sides of the nature of the world — or rather, science looks on the universe; religion looks in and through it.

So the true thinker takes with him, as no mean guide along with his intellect, his intuition. Out of their interaction, the thinker develops his religion. Nay, it grows in him. It is not so much a thing of syllogism, which would be like taking logic to a trysting place. It is the lover's recognition of his love. The first thing in the religion of thinking men is the immediate recognition of God. That makes anew their whole life. How poor is the man who says: Goodness is my religion, charity is my religion. It is as though he enjoyed the refreshing waters of the fountain, the while he carelessly sealed up the spring; as though while eating the fruit with gusto he burned the seeds. Action, call it even ethics, is not the primary manifestation of higher aspiration. First comes vision, desire, passion. First comes God. The world will not be redeemed by poor laws, not even by disarmament conferences. The accumulated wrongs of the ages will not be cleared out with electric fans. Not even with the fans of a hundred legislative enactments or relief agencies. None but God can redeem this world — God in the human heart, God softening the passions of man, transforming the stuff man is made of, rendering man as sensitive to the call of the spirit as an aeolian harp is to the wayward breath of the wandering wind. First God, a glad recognition, an overwhelming passion. Then *imitatio Dei*, the imitation of God, goodness.

The thinker passes from God to goodness very easily. The God who alone can explain and reconcile the world to us is a good and just and wise God. Surely such a God would want us, to whom He is united as parent to children, to be like Him. The highest conception of goodness that man can attain — that is God's demand of us. We neglect our God if we fail to live close to what we conceive God must be. We might offer sacrifices most painstakingly, offer our prayers daily, make our genuflections conscientiously, yet if we fail to subdue our heart into the image of God who should be there, we neglect our God. Conduct is the reflex of religion. It is the fruit of its tree, says the thinker. If there is no fruit, there is no religion; it is only farcical lip service. It is playing a part, and thinking that God will not find the player out. Not only will God discover him, but man also.

From the Father the thinker passes on to the children. Those who do not think, do not see the necessary consequence of the statement that God is Father. We are not only his children, but we are brothers, one to another. Love to the Father implies love to all his children. A glance at history will show how few have found the religion of thinking men, how few have found the brotherhood that unites us all, found it not only with our own kith and color, but with all the sons of men.

The thinking man knows that no force on earth passes away, is lost; that energy as well as matter is conserved, endures. And we are sure of nothing so much, it seems, as the vital energy within us, the power of hope, of love, the strength of endurance and the force of self-renunciation. Something titanic stirs within us; let us call it soul. The thinking man says that endures even after all things of the individual collapse and disintegrate. He will not say the manner of that life; he will not picture the details of that future existence, painted as they necessarily must be out of the pigments of his imagination. But he announces with unshakable conviction that the soul dies not. In fact, he finds that much that is inexplicable in life can be intelligibly explained only by positing immortality. He does not speak of a delicious heaven or a burning hell, but he speaks of a continuance of life beyond the grave.

So we see that the thinking man reduces very materially the credos of his faith. Almost does he say what the prophet of old said: "What doth the Lord require of thee: Only to do justly, and love mercy, and to walk humbly with thy God." He posits God as the heart of the world, and then justice, love, and humility. That is the religion of the thinking man. Thus simply he makes himself at home in the world. The simplest of faiths, the thinker's faith. How sure it makes him of life. When he steps out of doors and the heavens seem to be calling to him, in pensive blue or beckoning white, and God is abroad in the dust of the highway overlooking the ceaseless march of human feet, every breath becomes an act of worship, every thought an assertion of man's living immortality, and every feeling demands expression in actions of love and brotherliness. It is not that alone, this religion of the thinking man. There is in him the assurance of the oneness of God's life with man's life and with all life; it thrills from sky to sky, gleams in every star, sings in every bush, blooms in every flower, and blows in every breeze. Tears and pain and reft hearts become transfigured as part of the eternal love, and the sobs of man along with his laughter find their nest in the infinite heart.

The religion of the thinking man does not hide God behind the serried dogmas and formulae of the thousand denominations and religions, but finds Him revealed in our own heart and in the heart of our loved ones — revealed in the smile and frown of Nature, revealed in the song of birds and the beauty of flowers, revealed in the heroic courage and the simple observance of life's obligations shown by the faithful servants of the Most High. Catching a hint of Him in these many ways, the thinking man cries out: This is my God and I will adore Him, the God of my fathers and I will exalt Him.

PRAYER—THE VOICE OF RELIGION

A T THIS TIME of the year the urge for a national Day of Prayer is felt in many quarters, and when the news in the battle zones suggests a crucial situation, that feeling for national communion with God is intensified. Last year the National Council of Church Women called for a special prayer day, and this year the Governor of Texas in a proclamation set this day aside for public prayer by people of all faiths. Day of Prayer, World Day of Prayer! All who truly believe in prayer are favorable to such dramatic public petitions — if only there is a continuance of the practice of prayer daily. And that leads us to the consideration of the value of prayer. The whole subject needs careful and frank airing at this time, when an insistence on realism as against mysticism seems to have discouraged many in the exercise of prayer, when the so-called certainties of science crowd out and negate any need for lifting our hands and hearts to God. Science is King — almost the King of Kings — until we discover how science fails us in the tragic hours that are upon us and leaves us naked before the storm. Let us then discuss these related questions: Is prayer of value? Does it produce good results? Is prayer answered? How? What may be changed through prayer?

In many quarters prayer as the exercise of faith, the voice of religion, has fallen into entire neglect, and even has been considered an element of superstition. There will be many, therefore, who will shrug their shoulders and say, "What folly!" They will be apt to remember that when recently President Roosevelt told Madame Chiang

February 27, 1944.

Kai Shek that we will send China munitions, God helping us, she retorted, God helps those who help themselves. You see, they will say, our acts and efforts alone count. Science has taught us that the laws of the universe are immutable, that no mere utterance of a wish, even couched in the most eloquent and devout prayer form, can change the unalterable course of events.

Then, too, human pride and vaunting smugness and self-sufficiency have closed the doors of many hearts to the appeal of the soul through prayer which gave strength, courage, and comfort to the generations before us. Why ask God for favors when we can grasp all that we want without help from anyone? Why approach some Being above the stars to remake our world when we can do it so well ourselves? See how wonderfully we are steering the whole social world movement toward perfection in our own time! Yes, it certainly seemed to many that we needed no one to appeal to in this process of advancing world happiness and amity and welfare; we, ourselves, were lifting mankind to glorious achievement and undimmed happiness and certain security. So, the exercise of prayer was considered a sign of lack of self-confidence, in view of the fact that we had all the tools for human welfare well within our hands.

And then came another war, a world war, wider in extent and fought with more lethal weapons, and our self-confidence and smugness received a terrible shock. God, it seems, is still needed in this human world of ours — we will be constrained to ask His help in this dark hour of world tension, praying for wisdom amid the new complexities, for courage in the vast struggle, and for comfort when the shadow of untimely death appears in our homes. It is now, out of this destruction of the imposing structure which we built on what we thought was a sure foundation and in materials which we thought should withstand any onslaught — it is now that we discover that we cannot any longer remain smug and sure of ourselves. And so, we lift our eyes unto the mountain, unto God, whence cometh our help.

Is this a return to what so many people sneeringly dubbed medievalism? Is this treason to the human intellect? Is it a cowardly backtrack to obscurantism? When we admit with the Psalmist, "Thou dost light my lamp; The Lord my God doth lighten my darkness" (Ps. 18:29), does that deny the light of science and all the knowledges that have weaned us away from God and prayer? What is the lamp that God lights for us? What darkness does it illumine which nothing else can? And how does prayer bring that light to the lamp of our soul? Do you think that when Abraham prayed for Sodom and Gomorrah, when Moses prayed for his sister, Miriam, and for his people, when the Prophets and Psalmists called upon God, they were calling in vain and indulging in a foolish and futile exercise?

Let me state my belief that genuine, fervent, deep-felt prayer is answered. But how? The pagan conception of the relation of God to man was that man is a puppet of fate, utterly helpless in the grip of it — unless God would condescend to break the fetters with which fate had him bound. On the other hand, the Jewish conception of God's relation to man — and man's relation to God — was that man is a partner of God, an agent of God in the ordering of the universe. Just as God works through the forces of nature, so that they perform His will, so He also makes His plans to come true through the dreams and yearnings and the efforts of man.

Clearly this is the concept which the Psalmist conveys in his inimitable compendium of a people's prayer. To those who sneer that prayer is the effort of those supine souls who want to substitute God's intervention for the work of their own hands, the Psalmist has this answer, "May your heart be quickened" (Ps. 22:27). Prayer doesn't get the work done to obtain the result for which we ask, but it quickens our heart, it stirs our lagging spirit. It operates through the faith which it expresses — faith in God — to open the doors of action which before remained clogged by a hopelessness of better things. You have no doubt seen the working of the electric mechanism called the magnetic eye, which opens a door when someone's body comes near to shut out the light. Prayer is the magnetic eye operating in reverse; it opens the gateway toward the attainment of our goals when we put the light of God between us and it. It is the fashioner of the mood and the will toward that activity which will achieve what we so earnestly seek. The skirl of the bagpipes doesn't rout the enemy, but it infuses the Highland regiment with fiery courage that sends them on to a new assault of the enemy lines, an *élan* which nothing can stop or hinder or defeat. Thus prayer similarly stirs us to undreamed of persistence and unexpected effort to attack frontally and to attain that for which we prayed.

From this point of view, prayer is by no means a stopping of all effort while we raise our voice to God, asking Him for favors which we are too lazy to achieve by our own efforts. It is an exercise of the soul, the flexing of the spirit, as the athlete flexes his muscles before the leap into purposeful action. And that flexing of the spirit has three objectives, the first being concentration, putting the mind through prayer strenuously on the thing desired, and changing the petition from a purposeless cataloguing of petty little wishes into a sharply defined goal upon which our whole being concentrates. And from concentration, the prayer exercise proceeds to consecration of every faculty and resource to the end to be attained. From concentration and consecration, the prayer discipline rises to its climax in co-operation with the Divine through what modern psychology has termed "the reserve power of subconscious energy." The extent of that reserve power surprises us, for ordinarily we are not aware of its existence and therefore do not call upon it for the prosecution of that which is the object of our petition.

Ah, you say, that is all very fine — but what we effect by consecration, concentration, and co-operation through subconscious energy, is not the work of God answering your prayer, but comes through your own efforts. Exactly so — God always works through the laws of nature or the laws of our own human nature to attain His ends. Through the spiritual process of prayer we become the agents of God, we assume our rightful place as partners in that divine creative process. Without that spiritual force evoked by prayer many desired ends would be unattained.

But can't we obtain these results through other disciplines, through art, music, and poetry? Yes, those are fine disciplines and are often very effective, and they should be used by those who find them helpful for the cultivation of the spiritual personality. Prayer, however, is the peculiar and unique instrument of spiritual culture. It stirs the imagination like poetry; it stimulates aspiration like music; it quickens the finer sensibilities like love. In these times when destructive forces are abroad, when sure foundations totter and perils and uncertainties, heartaches and grief are very close to each one of us, prayer is the medicine of the soul; it reminds us of the Rock that stands firm, of the Father, the Comforter and Friend whose everlasting arms are around us amid all the darkness. God, may I add, can and I am sure often does answer prayer without using the agency of the human spirit — but in general man is included in the working out of prayer. To the person who asks: What will prayer get me? It is proper to answer with another question:

What do you want from it? Do you want it to give you financial security, to protect you from misfortune, to free you from trouble and responsibility, to guarantee you unmixed happiness? These things it cannot do.

But if you want to be properly adjusted to life, strong against bad fortune and able to stand good fortune without its going to your head, if you want to be alive to your duties, contented with your lot, able to find happiness even in the midst of unhappiness, then the answer is prayer, prayer every hour of the day, which can guide your actions toward moral ends. By teaching you how to live, by helping you relate yourself to God and to His Will, it offers you a way of life that has meaning and significance.

A world Day of Prayer — yes, by all means. And this would be my prayer:

Out of the depths we cry unto Thee, O Lord. The waters have gone over our souls and our heart faints within us. Where shall we turn when evil men rise up against us, destroying our peace and seeking to snatch away our loved ones and to deprive them of life and to take away our liberty and happiness? We can only turn to Thee who standest above the fury of the tempest and bringest light amid the dark places of the world.

We pray first of all at this time for that powerful agency of mercy, the American Red Cross, which is now calling upon us for the means to carry on its vast and manifold activities of helpfulness and compassion. In the midst of the brutal forces unleashed by war, it is the sign and symbol of the gentle and kindly and the humane. In the clash and rattle of murderous guns and bombs it speaks softly and acts swiftly in the mission of healing and nursing. Grant, O God, that we may gladly and fully respond to its call now. Bless Thou its work at home, in the camps, on fields of battle, among our men in prison camps, in the hospitals, wherever pain and suffering may be found. Help Thou the Red Cross in its missions of mercy.

We pray for all the storm-tossed and the sorrow-laden wherever they may be and to whatever race or nation they belong, whether they are of the two million of Israel, crucified and tortured in fiendish cruelty — helpless, hapless, unarmed men and women and children — or whether they are the ten million trampled under the relentless world war machine. We pray for the groaning populations in conquered lands, shackled slaves, starving and dying the slow and hard way. Our hearts grieve for those who mourn for loved ones who are gone; send Thou to their hearts the balm of Thy comfort.

And O Thou Father of us all, bring on the better day of peace on earth through justice and righteousness and brotherhood. May that peace come speedily when all who dwell on earth shall know that to Thee alone every knee must bend and every tongue give homage. May all created in Thine image recognize that they are brethren — not one the master and the other the slave — so that one in spirit and one in fellowship they may forever be united before Thee. Then shall Thy kingdom be established on earth and the word of Thine ancient seer be fulfilled, The Lord will reign forever and ever, when Thy name shall be One and all mankind One.

OUR FEAST OF TABERNACLES, Sukkoth, which was observed last week by the Jewish people throughout the world as it was celebrated in the Holy Land thirty centuries ago, has any number of lessons which it teaches most forcibly. It turns our thoughts to the tent of Israel which is in desperate straits in a number of lands. The winds of hate and the tempest of religious and racial prejudice, coupled with a cruel sadism which does not often affect an entire nation that has reached the high level of intellectual advance which Germany has attained, is toppling the Jewish tent in Germany into a Ghetto heap. And we seek some grain of hope from the Sukkah story. Is the pillar of cloud and the pillar of fire — divine guidance — still hovering over Israel's tent? But the Sukkah also calls for gratitude to God for the common, everyday blessings that are ours and reminds us of our duty to those who have not the gifts that have come to us; and above all it calls for optimism and trust in God. It assures us that no one can destroy Israel, except Israel itself.

Like the other symbolic Jewish festivals, the Sukkoth festival bears a universal message. The Sukkah or booth or movable hut which is the central symbol of the festival is certainly a symbol of the ideal home. It foreshadows what a home should be like, it is the model of the blessed domicile of the family. Let us try to decipher the lesson contained for all who would learn from this symbol. That it would be wise to spend some time and thought on the home and its amendment from the form it has taken in many places, few would be hardy enough to deny. The home, the physical center of the family, which is the nucleating cell in the system of our modern civilization, is disintegrating before our eyes, just falling apart. And following upon this breaking down of the home is the swift dissolution of the family, with a consequent deterioration in the morale of modern society.

The chain of events can easily be discerned in this line from broken homes to broken culture and destroyed civilization. The changed and altered homelife brings on family disruptions, with the divorce hopper turning out almost as many divorces in the large cities as the marriages which are, in the same time, recorded and solemnized. And broken homes and broken family life mean broken lives; family ties and family restraints and family supervision and solicitude are gone — and then follows the quick round of juvenile court, reform school, penitentiary, and confirmed criminality. And because homes have broken down, crime is prevalent in our land as never before. It behooves us, then, to think seriously again about the true home, the conditions that made it so strong a fortress against evil and a defense against temptation. For I think that by this time we have come to agree with that writer who stated his view of the supreme importance of the home when he said, "It matters not what a people cares for second or third, as long as it cares for its homes first."

And so I invite you to look at the symbol of the home as we find it in the Sukkah or booth or temporary hut which Israel was commanded to erect as part of the celebration of the Feast of Tabernacles. Very definite specifications were laid down for the kind of hut or booth or tabernacle that is to serve the purposes of this feast of thanksgiving. Beautiful and glowing though it may be, and most of these outdoor huts are gaily decorated by loving hands, the Sukkah must be a simple structure. So should our homes be, if they are to be wholesome. The mildew of social extravagance and the rottenness of proud ostentation are upon many houses which pass themselves off as homes. These great houses have none of the homeyness, the warmth and genuineness and ease and informality that should be an integral part of the real home. These high-ceilinged mansions, with their mullioned windows and their aping of a knightly period, now happily gone, these baronial castles obsolete in all their militant suggestions, these palaces that have no royalty residing in them or coming as guests may be mere examples of bad taste — if they are not used as homes. But if used as homes, they are utter frauds. They have none of the fundamental, necessary first elements of home — coziness, at-homeness, and genuineness. They hold aloft and blazon forth false values in that part of our civilization that should be most free of any kind of falseness. The stipulations as to the Sukkah or festal hut limited the height of it, that it be not the symbol of pride. Simple homes make true homes, informal and cozy and above all genuine, everything about them suggesting honest and true and eternal values.

And again the specifications of the festal booth, the Sukkah, state that it was to be but one-roomed. The suggestion is clear. The home is not a home if it be not a place of harmony. Only when parents and children walk together and live together, only when husband and wife and all members of the family group that are under one rooftree are united in the great and important things of life, of God and duty and truth and honor, can we speak of home. Let us hasten to add that this is not for a moment intended to intimate that there must be uniformity of thinking, that there is to be a dragooning of opinion, a dead gray monotony of what has popularly been called "yessing," with the curse of servility hanging over all of it. Yes, there is much room in the home for honest differences of opinion, for the earnest give and take of debate. But if in the fundamentals, in the deepest and most intimate points of outlook and hope and faith, in the very pit of our being, there is no harmony, then it is no home in the truest sense of the word. The routine of life may go along fairly smoothly, the inbred courtesy and decency may keep the house from tumbling upon the heads of the occupants, and even their pride may keep the festering sore of the discord of souls hidden from the public gaze. But as sure as man is a human being and not an angel, as sure as, in spite of all banter and cynicism, he yet has an inner kernel of conviction which will rise hostile against any fundamentally different kernel of conviction and outlook, the true inner harmony of that home is gone. A home may have different kinds of voices of different timbres and qualities and depths, but all the voices must sing in key, if it is to be a home. The key must be the key of God, the key of the good, the key of life's noblest sons. Only a harmonious home is a true home.

A further stipulation as to the Sukkah, the festal booth, is that it must be lived in for the period of the festal week. The home, too, must be lived in, not merely visited. The hearthstone must be the center of family life. One of the causes of the disintegration of the modern home is that no one is at home. The family is scurrying, in different and widely separate groups, all over creation. They appear everywhere, except at home. For many in the modern generation are trying to run away from themselves, from their own hollowness and emptiness, the very sight of which induces boredom. They do not think, they do not read, and they do not feel, so they have nothing to say to each other — and the family gathering becomes a dumb, dead, uninspiring, and inert group. No wonder that they shun the evening of the family at home. And yet unless such hearthstone gatherings occur frequently and at regular intervals each week, the home atmosphere dies of inanition.

The final stipulation as to the Sukkah is that it is to have no solid, permanent roof, it is to be ceiled with boughs of trees so that the stars may be seen from within. The home may be simple, and it may be harmonious and may even be a hearthstone home of a family that lives in unity, but if the stars are not visible it is not the perfect home. The stars! Of course, the meaning and intention are clear. It must have two final characteristics to be a real and blessed home. The stars — God must be seen in the home. There must be some very definite faith to which the home is dedicated and in which the name of God is called in reverence. Through such spiritual exercise the home receives the final glow of sacredness to beautify it. Don't smile so cynically, my friends, at home ceremonials of a religious nature. Those who have known what prayer at meals, kindling of the Sabbath lights, and similar ceremonials have meant to the home and to the young sprouts that spring from it, testify to its magic and transforming power. In the sunlight of religious home exercise, the little flowers of childhood grow into a finer beauty and a sturdier power. The stars — the home must be a place where the stars are seen, not just clod, where culture reigns, where ideas and ideals sprout thick and fast, and where high converse finds a hospitable reception.

The ideal home — like the Sukkah — must then be erected on the pillars of simplicity and genuineness, of harmony and beauty, of love and culture and faith. And as our homes approximate this ideal we will find that our young people will gain a new and finer depth of character and stronger faith, and will advance to fuller and more blessed achievements. Then instead of wise-cracking younger people, without conviction and without culture and without seriousness and without an earnest aim —

young folks so weak in character and so completely un-touched by nobility that they become utterly vicious with the first temptation — we will have a swift and happy response and a reaction toward those things that are the saving graces and virtues of human living, and our civili-zation will again proceed on its onward and upward way from the clod to the stars, from the animal and the beast unto the divine. But the road to that goal leads through the lovely, glowing rooms of the true and genuine and cozy and loving and reverent home.

REALITIES AND SHAMS OF SUCCESS

THE LARGEST PART of life is given over to a process of education whose ultimate aim is the discovery of the realities as against the shams. We seek it in art and in the sciences and in literature and in politics. It is the crux in religion. An unerring discrimination between the realities and the shams is the summation of life's wisdom. It is the philosopher's stone. The question with which we are told Pontius Pilate concerned himself, "What is truth?" is in essence the question. What is reality and what is sham? Life comes to us in so many guises that it is hard to decide what is real and what sham, or rather, the world comes to us so elaborately dressed that we have difficulty in separating the garment from the body, the sham from the real. What is passing and what is permanent, what is temporary and what eternal, what is the mode and what the substance, what is transient and what is elemental — this has been the problem of all religion, art, and science.

Dr. L. P. Jacks, the editor of the *Hibbert Journal,* in a recently published book called *Realities and Shams,* points out that realities have reserve and shams are blatant, loud, self-acclaiming; and no doubt this observation helps us in our discriminations. Use Dr. Jacks's plumb line to discover whether something in religion, art, literature, or science is sham or real, and it will not be so difficult a quest. Shams shout from the housetops, shriek for sensation; realities are reserved and self-contained. Why follow the will-o'-the-wisp sham, why bow down and sacrifice to the unreal, the false, and the vain if only by seeking and testing we may uncover for our devotion and service the real and substantial and permanent? Why bend the knee to Baal, when God may be seen on the mountaintop? Now and then we may be lured by the pipes of Pan, softening for a little while the hard day; now and then we may follow false yet pleasant trails; but surely in the end and in the important things we seek the great high road of duty and the reality of God.

Surely, then, we should put the matter of success to the test of "real" or "sham," for success bulks large in our strivings. It is almost a religion. In a recent article the Very Rev. William R. Inge, Dean of St. Paul's Cathedral, London, attempts to discover the religion of America. He points out that, although America has been the home of many cults and new religious groups, it is impossible to discover which is the religion of America, and insists that if any religion at all be characteristic of American life it is the religion of success, since to its shrine Americans of all denominations bring their votive offerings. Isn't there a great deal of truth in this diagnosis? It is true, it seems, that with the great majority of Americans the supreme goal is what is called success, that the supreme ideal motivating their lives is the ideal of attainment also designated success. So common is this quest with us, so seemingly universal seems its hold upon humankind, that we consider it a prime urge like hunger and fear. We think that it always was and that it is the ideal everywhere today. But, as a matter of fact, there are wide continents where the industrialism of the Occident has not gripped all life in its tentacles and absorbed all of the hopes and strivings of men, and in these great spaces success is not all. And let us remember that in the past it was religion that stirred men to great heroisms and called forth the greatest sacrifices and stirred men to dream nobly and held before them the great vision of a heavenly kingdom established upon earth, the vision of the City of God. In the past it was the great ideals of religion which called men to sacrifice and even to martyrdom. But today in America the high goal of life and of living has come to be the great god success. Should we not apply to it the test and discover what is real success and what is sham?

Toward what kind of success are most of us directing our efforts, frequently expending our last ounce of strength to attain it? Of course, there are slight variations, dependent upon individual characteristics and temperament, antecedents and training, but the common denominator is easily obtainable. If we turn to the business world the goal in that sphere is, when we view it frankly and without prejudice, the amassing of wealth; not the miser's passion for hoarding, but the desire for that which wealth gives and brings — comfort, position, recognition, and so on. And because business is the preponderant occupation of American life, the standard which it sets and the goal for which it aims become of necessity the standards and goal of the other endeavors. Thus even in the professions the standards of success have become wealth and position. The successful engineer is the wealthy engineer, and so the successful physician and the successful lawyer.

Even in the ministry, where wealth cannot truly be said to be the standard and the goal, the success of the individual is judged primarily by popularity and by crowds and by publicity attained, and only secondarily by character, earnestness, and a sense of consecration. And so, measured by this same commercial standard, lack of wealth or lack of popularity means that the minister is placed in the group of life's defeated ones and upon him is placed the stigma of a want of capacity. Often he is judged to be the handicapped, the weakling, the inferior. But is that a correct conclusion? What a sham such success is! How entirely unreal it is! It is blatant; it cries aloud and insists on being noticed and appreciated. Compared with the life of a certain friend of mine, who seldom enjoys a cigar because he can only afford a pipe, whose salary is just enough to keep him going, and who has yet done a wonderful piece of constructive work in the community in which he lives — creating there nothing less than a community conscience and a social intelligence — how shoddy and paltry is that kind of success whose index is money and position!

Material success is not unworthy, for without bread there can be no spiritual striving; without the physical elements the goals of the spirit are often impossible of attainment. It was in the glory of the Elizabethan reign that the greater glory of a Shakespeare could appear. But material success in and for itself, and standing by itself, is the veriest sham, and I am seeking to point out the folly of bending the knee to it. Not a success, but the saddest failure is the man who addicts himself to the amassing of wealth alone; one day he will sit beside his pile of gold and find it gives him no satisfaction and no joy; the uninterrupted pursuit of it has lost him the opportunity to make friends, to discover joys, to woo culture. He has all the gold, but as common parlance has it, "no place to go." Not a success, but the most tragic failure, is the one who has sacrificed even health to get on. Nerves gone, digestion broken down, what does his wealth mean to him? The irony of the situation is only paralleled by that of the man who has decided that he must take the view from the top of Mount Wilson, climbs up the steep height steadily, never turning aside to get rest or give a kind word or helping hand to other climbers, finds himself at last at the top of the mountain — and then, alas, discovers that he is stricken blind. That man is a tragic failure; he might have been a success had he stopped on the road to help other climbers — even though he had reached the top blind or had never reached it at all.

For real success is the success of service. It is the greatest of ideals. All other possible ideals — peace, justice, righteousness, happiness, joy, love — are all included in this one, since none of these is attainable except through the ministry and agency of this one ideal, service. I am thinking of service as a revelation of character. I am thinking of service as that which achieves character. I am thinking of the type of service that brings out those particular gifts with which most of us are endowed. He serves who "lives in the day, but not for the day," who reveals in his life an enthusiasm for men and a recognition of the spiritual essence of each and all men. He serves who gives of that of which he is capable, of all his gifts and all his endowments, of that which he might become through self-expression and self-development and constant devotion, gives these constantly and readily and places them on the altar of humanity to bless and inspire and ennoble mankind. Such men serve; and when they give the maximum of their service, give all of which they are capable, and give it in a high spirit, they have succeeded and theirs is success.

This being the reality of success, what is the way thereto? He who desires success of this kind must have a standard apart from those of the bloated Philistine, of the smug and complacent materialist; it must be the highest standard, it must be the greatest aim conceivable; it must be the noblest ideal thinkable. He must know himself. To attain real success you must know your powers, your capacities, your capabilities. You must know wherein your powers lie and you must not let any of them be wasted — you must use them to the fullest. And having a high standard, and knowing your powers, you must believe in yourself, believe in your potentialities, believe in your spiritual resources, and use them, develop them. Let what is in you come forth. Unfold yourself. Unfold all that is within you, for we are all full of "the germs of growth," and to fail to believe in these and develop them is treason to one's self and treason to our fellow-men, to whom our growth is also the only contribution and the only service that we can render.

Believe in yourself! The great souls of history have always been those who had such faith in themselves. In the first dawn of the world Abraham set a goal and an aim for himself; he believed in himself to the extent of being ready to forsake his home, his kindred, and his friends, and go out in search of the opportunity of self-realization and self-fulfilment. That was also true of Galileo; it was true of Marconi. We all stood about and laughed and jeered some twenty years ago at the Wright boys as they tried to fly into the air; but they believed in themselves and the airplane is with us. That has been true of every great discoverer and inventor, whether in the physical or the spiritual world. These have been the men who have had self-reliance and conviction and determination, and have dared to forsake the accepted and beaten paths, because they believed in themselves.

Then I say to you who would truly succeed, stand by, persevere; don't take a new tack, don't be veered off from your goal. Robert Louis Stevenson asked to have written on his tombstone the epitaph: "He clung to his paddle." And, lastly, let us remember what George Eliot advised, speaking in her figurative manner, "Don't take opium"; don't, as you march, permit yourself to be drugged by the flattery or praise of others, and don't let the opium of whatever wealth may come to you dull your sense and dim your vision of the higher aims and goals with which you began the journey. Be clear-eyed, clear-minded, true to yourself.

That is the real success, all the rest is sham. Wealth may come with that real success. It may not. Position and influence may be yours,too. But these are only incidental, for you will have succeeded only because you were true to your highest ideal, because you have given in service of the best that was within you, of your highest capacities, up to the fullest extent. It is a high aim, reaching out for this kind of success, when so many of those about us are intent upon the sham success. Failure may come, but let it not be defeat; for failure is but hope deferred, while defeat is hope lost.

Which one of these two men of whom the poet sings do you desire to be? It was a furious battle; men yelled and swords shocked upon swords and shields. A Prince's banner wavered, then staggered backward, hemmed by foes; a craven hung along the battle's edge and thought: "Had I a sword of keener steel — that blue blade that the king's son bears — but this blunt thing!" He snapped and flung it from his hand, and lowering crept away and left the field.

> Then came the King's son wounded, sore bestead,
> And weaponless and saw the broken sword,
> Hilt buried in the dry and trodden sand,
> And ran and snatched it, and with battle shout
> Lifted afresh, he hewed his enemy down
> And saved a great cause that heroic day.

One is the craven who always wants a sharp and shining sword; the sham success. Nothing else means anything to him — when he can't get that he slips out of the fight. But to the true prince even a broken, dulled sword becomes a weapon of real success, saving a great cause on a heroic day. Use whatever powers you have, broken though they be — use them with high aim, believing in yourself, use them to the fullest.

THE GIFT OF MEMORY FOR THESE TIMES

Remember the days of old, Consider the years of
many generations. Deut. 32:7.

HILE IT MAY BE TRUE that the fate of Lot's wife, when, according to the story, she changed into a pillar of salt, warns us against too persistent turning backward to the past — especially if that past is reminiscent of the sins of Sodom and Gomorrah — it is certainly wise for us to heed the appeal of Moses in his last song, his swan song to Israel, *Ha-azinu*. He urged the generation of the Exodus and of the perilous march through the wilderness, that much-tried generation of transition from slavery to freedom, to remember the days of old and to consider the years of many generations. To meet the present with stout hearts and level heads, to face the future with understanding and vision and with a hard realism tempered by a wise and clear-eyed optimism, we must have the guidance of the years that are gone. That we view the path on which we are setting our feet in proper perspective, that we judge our difficulties with a sense of proportion, that we employ historical knowledge for the avoidance of hysterical conclusions, that is the plea of the lawgiver. He calls us to look backward, to remember the past experience of mankind as we face the road before us. That road may not seem so utterly hopeless, so terribly uphill, so impossible to negotiate, when we recall the other roads taken bravely and traveled successfully in the many generations that went before us.

We have passed along a heartbreaking road — we and many other nations, most of them along darker and harder

December 5, 1943.

roads than we have had to undertake — during these past
few years. We are still in a crucial period of this war and
in a period of transition in the world's history. The storm
still breaks, the typhoon still sweeps across the world,
twisting the souls of millions upon millions of human
beings who have long suffered and are all too well
acquainted with grief. And most of us, realizing that mankind would be torn up by the roots in this cosmic storm,
are seeking to grasp some Eternal Rock, some assurance
that a righteous God liveth and that the world has not
been delivered over to blind forces and powers of evil,
and that the end of civilization, of decency, of righteousness is not inevitable.

Speaking to the world's anguish and despair, religion
has many heartening messages and assurances — if men
would only heed them, read them in the ancient book of
the Bible, and consider the years of many generations.
Permit me to suggest one such lesson, which may at this
time meet our sorest need. The admonition of religion
which I point out consists of but one word, *remember*.
Oh, the gift of memory! How precious it is — yet we more
easily forget than remember. "Remember the Sabbath
Day to keep it holy." Do we remember? "Remember what
Amalek did to thee." Do we remember? "Remember how
I walked before thee." Do we remember? "Remember
now thy Creator." Do we? "Remember the days of old,
consider the years of many generations." *Do we?*

Throughout the Great Book we hear the boom of the
reiterated command: Remember! The gift of memory is
very precious: it helps us taste the pleasures of life long
after they have passed our lips; it brings back the dear
features of those gone for a while; it preserves us from
the superficialities of today and the airiness of tomorrow
by giving us the depth and weight of yesterday; it tem-
pers the onrush of the present, and the allure of the

future, by the wise whispers of the past. Without the gift of memory we would be one-dimensional, unanchored, quick-flitting shadows in a bewildering world. It is in the Book of Deuteronomy, chapter 25, verses 17-19, that we read: "Remember what Amalek did unto thee by the way as ye came forth out of Egypt. . . . Thou shalt blot out the remembrance of Amalek from under heaven; thou shalt not forget." And the reason for this decree against Amalek is set forth: it is because Amalek "met thee by the way, and smote the hindmost of thee, all that were enfeebled in thy rear, when thou wast faint and weary; and he feared not God." Thus our memory is invoked; it may be the one gift that we need in these hard days.

Many of us have lost sight of certain facts that memory must serve up for us again. We are morally at sea, many of us, as we note the forces of evil in full sway, all that we consider fine and of good repute in the international life trampled under foot, and one nation after another battered into submission under the impact of a brutal war machine. Remember — remember why Amalek of old was successful, even though temporarily, in his raids on Israel, on the enfeebled and the faint and weary. Might it not have been partly Israel's fault? Because Israel had enfeebled itself? Wandering through the wilderness the people hungered after the fleshpots of Egypt, they went astray from the worship of God and danced around the golden calf, they murmured at the bitter waters of Meribah, always demanding sweetness and ease; they rebelled against their leader Moses and against all disciplined ways. In their disloyalties and their self-indulgences they had eaten away the marrow of their national strength and Amalek found them soft and weak, without the sustaining power of a great unshaken faith in God and goodness.

This world of today is facing its modern Amaleks who

are ravaging one nation after another. It has suffered immeasurably from the aggressor nations which seek to impose their authority and their economy and their way of life to the farthest reaches of the earth. The Amaleks, not fearing God, have taken away the life and liberty of one nation after another, have wrought havoc and imposed tortures upon women and children without a single qualm of conscience. For said they, "Pity and mercy are the virtues of the weak — and we are strong!" How swiftly marched the banners of these Amaleks across Europe conquering all, how thoroughly they loosed the tempest on the world! What massed suffering they caused! You come to your preachers and spiritual guides and ask them, with some asperity: Why and how is this possible in a world which you say is ruled by a good God? All I can say is, *remember!* These overwhelming successes of our modern Amaleks were brought about by the same cause that made Israel an easy temporary victim of those early marauders in the wilderness. The Amaleks of today also faced a generation weakened by its own self-indulgence and its lack of self-discipline. Most of all, the victim nations in this generation were bemused with an enfeebling unfaith, when they did not quite run amuck with a blatant cynicism and paganism. All through the world that spiritual disease had spread — and it was no wonder that some nations which had been trained to logical thoroughness should carry the unfaith to its extreme expression of deviltry and sadism.

Hate and cruelty, brutality and the last limit of savagery thus made the modern Amaleks successful, but we are all guilty and we must all repent. Let us not blame God; let us blame ourselves and our dancing around our golden calves, our hankering after the fleshpots of Egypt, our murmuring, and our demanding ease and good things without being ready to pay for them in the coin of honest dealing and self-discipline. *Remember!* Because our generation cared less and less for honor and duty and justice and kindliness and brotherhood, those nations that were thorough enough to remove all inhibitions along these lines carried their flags to the very last European democracy. Remember! Amalek of old learned the rudiments of lack of faith from the dancers around the idol, and bettered the lesson: they feared not God, and acted accordingly. Would we withstand the Amaleks? Then let us remember that the first sin was with all of us — and that sin must be atoned.

But the full import of that sentence in Deuteronomy also is needed today. *Remember Amalek* — how his name was blotted out from under heaven. Most of us fail to remember the teachings of history. If we did not so easily forget we would not be so utterly shaken and despairing when the Amaleks ride high. The Amaleks of history, those antisocial raiders and desperadoes, do from time to time strike a condition favorable for their technique and prosper accordingly, beating down the enfeebled and the hindmost, the faint and weary. The ensuing misery was explained by the prophets of Israel as the chastisement of divine Providence to remind a forgetting and loose world that God reigneth, to bring the haughty and pride-filled egotists to their knees — and to their senses — and to discipline an unregenerate age. But remember! The Amaleks all through the centuries had only their brief stay — and then their names were blotted out from under heaven, when an obstreperous generation had been fully purged.

Many of you think that the Amaleks have been successful all too long, and you have asked your spiritual guides, Where is thy God? I can only answer that God is where He has always been and doing what He has always been busied with: He is in the midst of this agonized world, healing, purging, and loving, so that the human race may make this world ever fairer with pity and kindliness, and mercy and justice, and honor and truth and brotherhood. Of course, if we children of His get out of hand the advance of human happiness is retarded and the Amaleks torture mankind. God is where He always is and the Amaleks and their machinations are not of His making. God bides His time, and in His own good hour the Amaleks are vanquished and their name blotted out from under heaven. All the Pharaohs and Ptolemys, the Sennacheribs and Nebuchadnezzars, the Alexanders and Caesars, the Alarics and Attilas, the Czars and Kaisers had their brief day — then their names were blotted out and their empires vanished with them and the anguish that they caused was soothed in a better day.

Only a week ago the death sentence of the Amalek of the East was announced at Cairo, and even now the same sentence on Germany is being decided at Teheran; and when peace is finally achieved we may forgive — our religions so command — but we must not forget. That would be fatal! *Remember* — Thou shalt not forget! And it will soon come to pass that our faith has been rewarded and all the multitudinous sorrows and pains and tragedies of these days will be adjudged as the birth pangs of a new age. Can we not make it a better, a more civilized and decent age? An age in which those precious things that make life worth living, human dignity and human liberty and human responsibility, shall be firmly established, an age of true democracy and true religion founded on freedom and human equality, on justice and brotherhood. If that age comes soon, even the bitterest of tears that have been shed these past few years will have been worth while, for they will have washed away the sin of unbelief, of little faith. God speed that better day!

184

TREASURES DISCARDED

hOW FREQUENTLY do we fail to reach the inner wisdom of a great sentence in the Bible because we are busy trying to prove or disprove the historicity of the statement. One such statement is found in the fourth chapter of Exodus; when God sends Moses to Pharaoh to demand the enfranchisement of the Hebrew slaves, and to the slaves themselves to apprise them of their imminent freedom, Moses objects saying: " 'But, behold, they will not believe me, nor hearken unto my voice; for they will say: The Lord hath not appeared unto thee.' And the Lord said unto him: 'What is that in thy hand?' And he said: 'A rod.' And He said: 'Cast it on the ground.' And . . . it became a serpent; and Moses fled from before it. And the Lord said unto Moses: 'Put forth thy hand and take it by the tail' — and he put forth his hand, and laid hold of it, and it became a rod in his hand." That is the story of the Rod and the Serpent. How much time and energy and how many words have been spent on the futile discussion as to whether the rod did indeed turn to a serpent and then back to a rod, whether the rod in turning to a serpent had yielded its "very" nature — the word "very" in the sense of substantial is being overused in the present day religious (or shall I say irreligious?) arguments! — and then some more time is spent upon the rehearsal of the hoary old discussions on miracles. And through the murk of this kind of discussion the real wisdom of the passage remains unrevealed.

Whether the incident mentioned in the fourth chapter

February 2, 1941.

of Exodus is historical or not, it is in the best sense of the word true; whether it is a miracle or not, it is the very essence of life. To the frail mortality of mankind a certain number of magic rods have been given to fend off the evil spirits and the thousand perils that crouch at man's door and dog his steps through life. They are the staves with which he feels for the pitfalls of the road as he walks his destined three score and ten or mayhap four score years, and upon whose strength he may lean his weight when weary of the long journey. God has been good and has given mankind many such rods, and amongst them are knowledge, truth, reason, religion, justice, honor, and love. These rods of God make the long journey of life not only a tolerable but a truly pleasant one, because it is an intelligible adventure. They keep us with our faces and our eyes to the stars; they restrain us from wallowing in the mire as a thousand calls from the flesh invite us to do. They sit on the brute within us and evoke the angel of our soul. If you cherish and foster these rods, as many a man does his less useful and more or less ornamental walking sticks, though they may not help you to wealth and power, they will give you the serenity and self-respect without which happiness is but the ghost of its reality.

But if you cast them aside, discarding them as so much hampering baggage on your road (along the "primrose path of dalliance"), then they become hissing serpents which sting with a deathly venom. Nothing is more tragic than the abasement to lies when one has known truth intimately; nothing more awful than the espousal of hate when one has been wedded to love; nothing more low than the surrender to injustice when one has bent the knee to the majesty of decency and law and order; nothing more fearsome than the darkness of unbelief when one has once walked in the lighted garden of the world

with God. The denial of the better and the acceptance of
the worse is a veritable serpent. (And sometimes the
gruesome tragedy involved in this desertion of knowledge
and justice, of truth and God, comes home to those who
have discarded the rod and found the serpent; many of
these have learned the lesson which the story in Exodus
teaches, that you can again take hold of the discarded
rod that had become a serpent — and if that is done with
faith and with courage you have your rod again, never
to be discarded.)

All about us things are being discarded that a former
generation treasured. Of course, each generation had
some things to throw away that cluttered up its house,
broken furniture that had once been useful but which
was now beyond repair. But it seems as though our generation has discovered an atticful of old and useless stuff
that can never be of any use to mortal man, stuff that the
inertia and the indolence and sometimes the reverence of
previous generations refused to throw out. And we of the
twentieth century have been in a very fury of house-
cleaning. The attic must be cleared of these cobwebbed,
dusty, forgotten things. And I believe enough in sanita-
tion to admit that the general principle is right, though
many of us can recall the accident when something very
precious was thrown out with the dustings. While desir-
ing to clean up let us beware of throwing out the baby
with the bath.

To change the metaphor, I think it is good for our
mental honesty and spiritual integrity to make our adjust-
ments in the matter of belief and attitude according to
the added light that has filtered into the world and into
our soul in the course of the years. Why should we constantly bruise our shins falling over a worm-eaten whatnot
which stands unused and in the way; it has been superseded; throw it out. But sift, search, discriminate. Many

a jewel has been thrown into the dustbin. Just as all is not gold that glitters, so all is not dust that has slipped into the attic. Many things that were helpful rods have been discarded in these days, and we have not only deprived ourselves thereby of the support of the staves, but we have left ourselves defenseless before the serpents which have taken their place.

Let us take account of some of the things that this generation is so gaily discarding. Well, the ceremonials of religion — no matter what the religion — are being shabbily treated these days. They are said to smack of medievalism, of something older than that; as if such a charge involves something dangerous and criminal. Does age perhaps imply moral turpitude? The mental equipment of man is such that it does not readily adjust itself to abstractions. Euclid's abstractions require diagrams, the age-old Euclidean figures of triangle and circle, of rectangle and square. So the abstraction of space was made concrete and gained entry into the human mind. The abstraction of Divinity needs that kind of concreteness to be apprehended by us. An Einstein, a Newton, a Galileo may be able to think fluently in abstractions, but there are not five men in a generation who can do that. We need concreteness, which in truth compromises on certain matters, but without which the abstraction would certainly remain unapprehended. Ceremonial is the yielding to the human in us, to the finite and the mortal; it arises from the recognition of human limitations. Man in his march toward God, man in his yearning for apprehension of the Divine Presence, must use the crutch of ceremonials. But, say our modern hotspurs, it's a crutch; throw it away. And the thing itself, the abstraction which cannot be reached by us without the crutch, remains unperceived, the Divine Presence does not appear.

Religion itself is also being bodily thrown out as so

much cluttering stuff in many quarters. There are those who say that science has made religion unnecessary. I wonder how. Can they tell? Does science say a single word about the First Cause? Has it discovered how things came to be in the very beginning? What cogency is there in the mechanistic argument? Has science told us how honor and duty and love came to be? The young sophomore with his little smattering of the odds and ends of science is blinded into his callow atheism, but the real student of science knows even science's limitations and beyond the veil sees God. To the student of science God becomes ever greater and more powerful and more necessary the more science reveals; as one of them said, "My God, I think Thy thoughts after Thee." While you are throwing the cluttering things that were once called religion out of your way, be careful that you do not cast aside the one explanation of this universe that truly explains, that you do not discard the one hope and comfort in this trying valley of life.

And with the casting aside of ceremonials of religion and faith itself, the things that naturally go with them are also discarded. Modesty and sobriety of conduct seem to be going fast. People now speak with a sneer, or at any rate with an air of condescension, of the Mid-Victorian era, and Mid-Victorianism is anathema to the gay young modern. Well, what is Mid-Victorianism? What are some of the characteristics of the Mid-Victorian age? By the way, we are not speaking of any prehistoric era; it was only yesterday, as it were; the day of our grandparents at the farthest. Queen Victoria ruled in England almost throughout the entire nineteenth century; Lytton Strachey in his fine biography tells pretty near all that can be said of that period, even though he doesn't say it quite sympathetically. Perhaps he too is smitten with Mid-Victoria-phobia.

One thing stands out in the efforts of Victoria's reign: she decided that her court should not be like those of the rest of Europe, a place of profligacy, nor would she countenance such profligacy in any way. No lady smirched by even the slightest breath of scandal could be presented at her court. That was sneeringly called the Rule of Respectability — not so bad a rule, is it? And the character of the British did not suffer because of the imposition of uncompromising morality. He is still the gallant Englishman standing bloody and bruised behind the Dover Cliffs — but unconquered! But now Mid-Victorianism is out of date, as much as the stiff, horsehair Mid-Victorian furniture that many of us remember as having long stood in solemn ugliness in our parlors until someone had the effrontery or good sense to throw it out. Of course our attitude to morality should not be affected by our attitude to the furniture or art of any given period. But we have thrown out, some of us, Mid-Victorian decency and modesty and respectability with our horsehair furniture. In the same way we discarded discipline and self-control and told our children to express themselves. And the discarded rod has turned to the serpent. Its slime and venom are even now poisoning the generation of today.

And whole nations have discarded the staff of life and it became a hissing serpent. Consciously and blatantly Germany and Russia — Nazi and Communist — discarded religion and all its implications and inhibitions; and Italy in Fascist ranks less obviously though none the less effectively did the same thing — and this defection set them on the road of this era of revolutionary and destructive war. Paganism, in the saddle there, is seeking to unseat justice, mercy, truth, and righteousness and all that the religious culture has demanded, because those high considerations of religion stand in the way of their program of force to the uttermost. As with the individuals, so with nations, the discarded things will become the hissing serpents. In fact they have already become so, poisoning the lives of millions and bringing slavery and torture, despair and death unto our world.

I am sure that in the Inferno which Dante pictures there must have been a most terrible and lurid place where people feverishly search for the precious things which in their folly they threw away during their lives. For a moment let us peep into some such Inferno. There go that numerous and ever increasing band of men and women — rather mostly boys and girls, young criminals who are infesting our cities and our highways and whose tragic end is bound to be a violent one. They threw away the rods that I spoke of — and there they go, one of the saddest spectacles of modern life. Then there is another group. Look at them, they seem gay and carefree, but if we look closely we will see how forced all of that is. There is no inner joy in them, just a surface glitter — not brilliant, just brilliantine. That group — so utterly joyless and aimless, who laugh at the very words "to be earnest, to be loyal and to be true to the best self," has gotten to this pass in the Inferno because it became wedded to the secular view of life which says there is no God, no such thing as conscience, which laughs at inhibitions of all kinds, which denies all restraints and self-discipline. And as with individuals, so with nations.

Let that Inferno of the discarded ideals not come into our life or the life of America, as a nation. Let us value our rods aright. Impedimenta must go so that civilization shall progress. But let us hold fast to honest and kindly human relations, to democracy and faith in God. Let us keep our rods, these things that have been the staff and support of the generations past, that have been their guide and their stay — modesty and sobriety of conduct, self-discipline and self-restraint, knowledge, truth, faith, religion, justice, and love — and they will be also rods unto us to support us on the long and hard road.

THANKFULNESS—THE FINE FRUIT
OF GREAT CULTIVATION

And when Daniel knew that the writing was signed,
he ... prayed, and gave thanks before his God, as he
did aforetime.   **Dan. 6:11.**

THE STORY OF DANIEL, as told in the twelve brief chapters after the Book of Esther, is one which is often used as the basis of chronology to discover the time of the end of the world. To me that has always seemed a futile effort and an utter waste of good time. Those who engage in it frequently disregard and are forgetful of the fine common sense of many lessons in the book, of the high courage of Daniel and his companions and of his rugged faith and moral resolution. In the incident of which our text speaks we are told that a conspiracy threatened his career and his very life; and when his enemies "came tumultuously" to complete their triumph over the righteous man they found him praying and giving thanks before his God "as he did aforetime."

Our American Thanksgiving Day these last three years has come when we find ourselves confronted by nations which have come tumultuously against us, planning one of the wickedest and most far-reaching and ambitious conspiracies of history for world domination. It also comes at the time when we must sadly count our casualties by the half-million, when some two million of our armed forces are in the midst of the hardest fighting at the Siegfried line and in Leyte, which campaigns are perhaps without compare in the military records of all times. And yet we, like Daniel with the windows of our soul open

---

November 26, 1944.

unto God, pray and give thanks. Like Daniel, facing an evil conspiracy and a desperate and monstrous threat against our national life and world order we, as a nation, offer prayer and thanksgiving; and perhaps we do this more fervently and sincerely and devoutly than in piping days and years of peace and world tranquillity. As with Daniel, such response and such reaction to the hostile forces round about is the result of wise and spiritual nurturing. Adversity neither cows nor bitterly enrages, but strengthens the hands and stiffens the determination to resist and ennoble the soul. Like Daniel, faced by tumultuous men, we pray and thank God.

Gratitude is the grace note of mankind. Like every fine and desirable fruit of the human soul, it requires long and careful cultivation in a threefold process. Thankfulness must be expressed; it means as much to him who brings thanks as to him to whom they are offered. To accept the gifts of kind hearts and stolidly to remain silent not only threatens to dry up the source of goodness, but coarsens the silent soul. Let us thank God and good men and women when we are the recipients of favors. Thus we cultivate the fine fruits of gratitude. And we also need vision to cultivate gratitude, that we may see the many and overwhelming reasons for gratitude, that we may not feel so utterly disgruntled at the failure to receive some gifts which we thought were necessary for our happiness, and that we may not take for granted without any acknowledgment those favors which are bestowed on us. Let us count all our blessings — even the commonest — and see how wonderful they are, and so give zest to our thanks. And then, for the proper cultivation of the fine fruit of gratitude we must employ what wisdom is granted to us to enable us to realize that the denial to us of some of the things for which we yearn may be, as at times we unmistakably discover, a blessing in disguise.

It is in these ways that we cultivate the fine fruit of gratitude. Samuel Johnson was right when he said: "Gratitude is the fruit of great cultivation. You do not find it among gross people."

So in the midst of a devastating war, at what may be its very climax, while our hearts are torn with a thousand anxieties, let us truly count all our blessings. And first and foremost let us recognize and devoutly thank God for our commonest, daily blessings, for the sunshine and the evening glow, for all the loveliness of nature in all its phases, for health and strength, for home and love, and for friendship. Because these come in such abundance and are the daily gifts which we enjoy they should not therefore be taken for granted. They are nonetheless blessings for which we should never fail to be grateful. How quickly we miss them and yearn for them and pray for them once we are deprived of them — of our health, of our loved ones, of our eyesight or our hearing, of the many joys that come through the pleasant gateway of our senses. Once we are denied the joy of the songbirds' twitter, the glow of the morning sunshine, the laughter of children — the tender words and the devoted attention of loved ones — how empty our life becomes! Let us thank God for the common daily gifts that are so generously and bountifully ours every day.

Let us thank God for this our glorious land, America, this surprisingly abundant land, with its vast resources, its wide and far-stretching boundaries, its rich harvests and ever renewed fertility. Above all, we must thank God for the continuing functioning of democracy and its ability to perfect itself, and for the right-thinking of the masses of our citizenry which knows that even the Constitution of the United States needed and was improved by changes and amendments. We thank God for the depth of indignation which has swept through our land, even though it came belatedly, indignation hot and furious at the tyranny and cruelty of the enemies of society in Germany, Italy, and Japan. We thank God that the old fervor for freedom still glows in the breast of every American worthy of the name — and that the torch of the Statue of Liberty still burns undimmed though many adverse winds arising from Nazi malignant vaporings would seek to extinguish it.

And let us thank God for the heritage which is America's, a heritage that has come from many lands and belongs to all the strands of human migration which, coming here to this blessed land, are now united in one indissoluble bond. We think of that heritage today — at the Thanksgiving season — because the origin of this national festival is found in the reverent act of thanksgiving of the first of these arrivals on the American shore, the Pilgrim Fathers. The ship that brought them here — like those other ships that carried to these shores other seekers for security and liberty — brought part of America's heritage — a noble part. What is that *Mayflower* treasure which is now the American heritage? First of all among the treasures of the *Mayflower* is the pioneer spirit, the fearlessness and the sturdiness that enabled its people to conquer and subdue a continent. These men of the *Mayflower* were no milksops who feared labor. They were not primarily set toward ease. They loved nature, the lonely moors, the silent forests, the long fertile plains. They were hardy people who cared not for the frivolity of a Sodom, but were willing to live in the solitudes of Zoar, if only they could live with their God. They were not afraid of the silences. Out of their loins came the great pioneers who conquered the Ohio Valley, who touched the reaches of the Mississippi, who went with Clarke into the great Northwest, and with Austin to Texas. From their seed came the simple pioneering families who built America out of a silent, untamed continent, faithful to

196

the evangel of work and the indefatigable spirit of the conquest of nature. And we thank God today for that spirit.

Another treasure of the *Mayflower* is the Bible. Though it may be that no Jew came in the *Mayflower,* as he did in the *Santa Maria* with Christopher Columbus, his spirit and his Book did come. The Old Testament appealed to the congregation of the *Mayflower.* They made its theocracy a guide for the government that they set up. Dr. Samuel Langdon, one of the earliest presidents of Harvard College, in a speech before the Congress of Massachusetts Bay on May 31, 1775, taking his text from Isa. 1:26, "And I will restore thy judges as at the first," said, "The Jewish government according to the original constitution which was divinely established, if considered merely in a civil view, was a perfect republic. The civil policy of Israel is doubtless an excellent model, allowing for some peculiarities; at least, some principal laws and orders of it may be copied in more modern establishments."

They were steeped in the Old Testament, they lived its life, they spoke its words. God was as real to them as to the Bible people. They brought a strong Biblical trust and faith with them, and withal they had a real respect for the Bible folk, the Jews, the people of the Book. And they brought a yearning for political and civil liberty, as no other section of the pioneers of this country did; certainly no other section yearned for it so greatly. The compact which they signed at the beginning of the voyage, the famous Mayflower Compact, showed that they were versed in self-government, that they had already practiced it in Holland, and that they had the virtue of self-mastery without which there can be no real self-government. Under their governor, William Bradford, they truly governed themselves on the broadest principles of democracy. The very seeds of the Constitution

197

came over in the hold of the *Mayflower*. Let us thank God for the Bible and its moral and spiritual direction of our American way of life.

But the greatest treasure of all in this cargo of the *Mayflower* was the insistence on religious freedom. It was the demand for religious liberty that drove the people of the *Mayflower* to Holland twelve years before their voyage westward. They were bent on worshiping God according to the dictates of their conscience. In England they would not accept the minister whom the bishops sent them. They wanted to be free to worship as they pleased. They refused to have their conscience governed by an established church. And we do not hesitate to say that just as religion in our opinion is the most important sphere of man's soul, so this insistence on religious liberty is the greatest and most precious treasure the *Mayflower* brought here. It was that treasure that put the general spirit of toleration and mutual respect into the character of our democracy, just as it placed into the Constitution as its first amendment the provision that "Congress shall make no law respecting the establishment of religion, nor prohibiting the free exercise thereof." It is the keystone at which organized groups in our land have recently been aiming their bludgeons of ignorance and intolerance, all the while claiming for themselves the only, original, and undiluted Americanism. Let us point this heritage out to those who seek to set one group of Americans against another group, fostering here the hatreds and suspicions which have caused the downfall of so many nations in Europe. We need union above all — not division and divisiveness.

Thank God for America. Here it is in the *Mayflower* spirit and the spirit of those other great and little ships that brought, most of them in the steerage of the immigrants, the culture and love of liberty to these shores:

the clean, frugal, sturdy pioneer spirit which loves the simple life and God's great out-of-doors; the Bible and the sense of nearness to God; the love for and devotion to political liberty; and the passion for religious freedom. May our Thanksgiving prayer be that America may grow into its great destiny, out of the life and death struggle in which we are now locked, that it will continue to hold its place as the land of light amid the outer darkness, as the true land of promise, the pearl of great price which God lifted out of the Atlantic.

AT THE CROSSROADS:
THREE QUESTIONS, ONE ANSWER

"Then said I to the angel that spoke with me: 'Whither do these bear the measure?' And he said unto me: 'To build her a house ... and she shall be set there in her own place.'"   Zech. 5:10, 11.

HEN THE LATEST and most destructive war in history ended with the surrender of Germany and Japan most people thought that the victory of the Allies on the fields of battle had set all things aright and that normal ways of peace would immediately follow. But wars and victories do not settle anything, except that they decide who for the time being was the stronger — in this case, the Allies or the Axis. Since those victories and surrenders the world has continued to be seriously disturbed, and turbulence appears in a number of lands. Our men in the armed forces are returning home in ever larger numbers, and they are wondering whether the things against which they fought have really been defeated and the ideals for which they sacrificed so much have really won out. They are coming home disillusioned and disheartened, and many of them are just plain mad — as they tell us in newspaper interviews and magazine articles. It is about time that we all realized that civilization is at the crossroads and that men and nations must seek and take the right path.

In this serious world situation I turned to my Bible and sought out the writings of the prophet who said, "But it shall come to pass, that at evening time there shall be light." Perhaps one who thus confidently spoke

---

November 4, 1945.

200

of hopeful ending of gloom and darkness would have a helpful word for this turbulence abroad in the world. So I opened to the prophecy of Zechariah.

The prophet Zechariah is called a minor prophet, but in the fourteen chapters of his book he presents most important and pertinent messages to his generation. That generation had experienced the sufferings and the heart-ache of the Babylonian exile, and it was the function of this seer to explain to his people the cause of their misfortune and the way toward the permanent establishment of their peace and happiness. His messages were given in the form of eight visions, and our text is found in the vision described in chapter 5. There he evokes the picture of an ephah, a measure or receptacle capable of containing some thirty-nine quarts, in which sits a person carrying a disk of lead weighing as some commentators suggest a talent, or a hundredweight, and then we read the explanatory phrase, this is Wickedness. Two winged angels (and "the wind was in their wings") take the ephah or heavily weighted measure containing a personification of Wickedness or Iniquity, and when asked, "Whither do these bear the measure?" they say, "to build her a house ... and she shall be set there in her own place."

It is a most unusual and perplexing vision and may mean a number of things. There were some Biblical prophets who resorted to rather complicated visions to announce their messages; but this may be said of them, as of all the prophets of the Bible, that though they had in mind to foretell what they were certain would happen in the near future as part of the destiny of their generation or the one after it — thus giving only a temporally significant prophecy or foretelling — the important part of the prophecy or the forth-telling was an indictment of the people for the evil, the wickedness, or the iniquity which brought on the people's misfortune and a clear and impassioned statement of the method whereby the evil decree might be voided and a better age be brought into being. Herein lies the high value of the utterances of the Biblical prophets: not in their foretellings, but in their passionate rebukings of the wickedness of their age and their plans for moral regeneration. That twofold prophetic teaching is their great and superlative message to all ages, universal and eternal in its application.

For our time this vision of Zechariah casts a most revealing illumination on the preplexing obscurity which pervades all the present human relations in our personal, national, and world affairs. Perhaps there never was a time when so many seemingly insoluble and disturbing and perplexing problems have risen all at once to plague mankind. They are the heavy disk of lead, the ephah or measure, and the figure of Wickedness which the vision of Zechariah discloses. This is the monstrous modern burden which this generation bears upon its straining shoulders. Who are the wise men and women to open up the ephah that Wickedness may be exorcised and that the leaden burden may be molded into that beneficent material which will, in the very spirit of the prophet, build a house which shall be established and set upon a firm base?

First of all the ephah, the receptacle of Wickedness and all its heavy burden, must be opened. Let us know and see and understand the oppressive burdens which bear us down. Any one of them may crush this age into another blackout of war and perhaps of annihilation, any one of them is so immediate and pressing that we must be apprised of its peril now. We are at a crossroads such as has appeared only a few times in the story and destiny of the human race. Let us examine the situation, so that we may choose the right road. What are the disks of lead that bear us down? What is the burden of this age? There are first the small fires of international battles raging in China, in Indonesia, and elsewhere which may flame into devastating conflagrations. There is the heavy task of reorganizing the German and Japanese governments so as to render them innocuous as fomentors of world disturbance. There is Russia, the portentous "X" in the planning of the international questions, unknown to many of us and suspected and feared. The whole of Central Europe is part of the world burden, and Poland and Hungary and Rumania and the Balkans are its uncertain factors. There is the turbulent Middle East which may explode any day if and when England or France, the United States or Russia creates the spark. There are the seething mass of displaced persons and the tragedy of hunger in most of Europe which weigh upon the conscience of mankind. And there is the futility of the London meeting for the United Nations Organization — and over it all there is the atomic bomb, and the entrance of the world into the unpredictable Age of Atomic Energy.

Here at home, in the face of much-needed reconversion to assure the returning veterans of employment, the growing feud in the relations of labor and employer groups is part of the heavy burden. At this time, too, on the twenty-eighth anniversary of the Balfour Declaration, the plight of the Jewish victims of Nazi cruelty who are kept from entering Palestine by the restrictions of the White Paper, as well as the growing turbulence between the Jewish Yishuv and the Arabs, are grievous burdens in the ephah of global perils. When we thus list these many world danger signs, when we enumerate and weigh them one by one — though we have brought out from the receptacle only the most ominous — we see in what a parlous state the world finds itself. After the sigh of relief at the end of the war, we discover that the bag of global evil has by no means been emptied through the sacrifice of millions of men, women, and children.

There are three fundamental questions which are in the minds and often on the lips of thoughtful people, who cannot live by the day and the hour, but must by their nature and serious thought look ahead if only for a generation. The first question is on the level of the individual, the community, and the relation of groups of people with each other. It has to deal with the intolerable animosities which have again so soon after the close of the war raised their baleful heads; radical and religious hostilities fostered not only by the Gerald L. K. Smiths and the Joe McWilliams's, but even by rabble-rousers in our national legislative halls. The first question is: *Must men hate?* When we have just finished a war in which each group, each religious and racial division gave its sacrifice of men and treasure, must men hate?

The second question is on the level of national governments. The serious disturbances in economic lines, the whole problem of providing a decent standard of living, the vital matter of full employment, and the very pressing issue involved in the increasing controversies between labor and management in which the general public finds itself always at a disadvantage, all these items of embroilment raise the second question: *Can democracies function wisely and efficiently?*

The third question is on the level of world affairs, of the destiny of the nations as they face each other in an ever contracting world. Neither vast oceans nor spacious land areas separate one nation from another in these days when airplanes make the trip from Tokyo to Washington in twenty-seven hours. We are all more or less living in one room, and what one nation does or plans affects the welfare of every other nation. When the British Colonial Office remains adamant on the retention of the restrictions on Jewish immigration into the Holy Land because it fears the Arab League; when suspicions between nations become more and more drastic; when Russia, Great Britain, and the United States fail to reach any conclusions on important international questions about the Balkans, Rumania, Hungary, Greece, and the Middle East; when the whole structure of the United Nations Organization is left in mid-air because no agreements that are central to world organization can be reached; then, with the atomic bomb and the Atomic Age before us, things look dark globally. The third questions is: *What of the Charter and what of world federation?*

The vision of Zechariah sees and understands the danger of the heavy leaden weight of world troubles, and it has but one answer: to build a house, which shall be established and set on a firm base. You can't build a house in your city, or the nation, or the world unless you apply some cohesive material, the binding mortar or connecting girders which hold together the various elements with their differing qualities. Cast out the wickedness of selfishness and greed and covetousness and hate and suspicion, put a quietus on the rabble-rousers and the cheap and noisy demagogues, cast out the desire for world dominance, cast out the spirit of exploitation of the weaker by the stronger — and then we can start to build the house of humanity, the United World Organization which with the years will become stronger and ever more effective. But the important thing is to start to build instead of tear down, to devote ourselves prayerfully to putting together the full force of the agencies of brotherhood. Then, at the crossroads, in the face of the Atomic Age, the House of Man will be established making beneficent use of the power inherent in atomic developments, so that life shall be ever more and more abundant and shall be set upon the firm base of justice and righteousness.

TWO HISTORIC REFUSALS

I T WOULD BE exceedingly interesting to study the cases in history where "No" was a decisive answer, and where "Yes" may have changed the whole face of history. It is not my intention to do that this morning, but just to state a few such instances of the historic No, and then proceed to the consideration of two exceptionally great refusals — two negatives which any of us might offer to some concrete challenge — and their significance in our lives.

The first and second No come readily to mind, and certainly they were historically decisive. One was the No of the Jewish people when asked to give up their God and worship the Greek gods at the time of the Maccabees. The second No was given by the same people when they refused at the rise of Christianity to recognize any divinity outside the One God. Through the first refusal, Israel preserved Judaism, which otherwise would have been submerged in Hellenism; through the second, they preserved monotheism — though they also accepted two thousand years of tragic Jewish suffering thereby. Pharaoh said No when commanded to liberate Israel — and Pharaoh and Egypt were punished. Then of course, we think of Gideon's No when he was offered the kingship, and the No of Cincinnatus, the patrician farmer who, after saving the Roman army under the Roman Consul Lucius Minucius, refused to continue his twenty-one-day dictatorship and went back to his plow.

In this connection we cannot help thinking of the No with which George Washington answered those of his counsellors who urged him to seize the hereditary kingship over the colonies which were forming themselves into a Confederation after the Revolutionary War. And then we think of the No of the Czar of Russia when he was asked from time to time for liberal laws for his people. And the No of Dollfuss, Chancellor of Austria, comes to our mind, the No to the demand that he capitulate to the Hitlerites and the Nazis and unite with them in all their policies. The latter two refusals — the same word No — brought death as the penalty to both the Czar and Dollfuss, but how different is their place in history! The Czar died amid calumny, Dollfuss as a hero.

But now let me turn your attention to two exceptionally challenging and most instructive refusals in Bible history. The first occurs in the midst of a rebellion against the authority of Moses. Korah, the son of Izhar, the son of Kehoth, the son of Levi — therefore of the select tribe — as we read in the sixteenth chapter of Numbers, gathered together a band of discontented persons, with Dathan and Abiram, 250 men, princes of the congregation, the elect men of the assembly, men of renown. Moses wanted to confer with Dathan and Abiram and others of those who had been misled by the rebel Korah, so as to set them right in the important matter of communal management and authority. They refused to come, saying "*Lo Na-aleh,* we will not come up." It was a decisive and historic refusal, for Korah, Dathan, and Abiram and all that host of princes of the congregation and elect men of the assembly, men of renown, were destroyed. "The earth opened her mouth, and swallowed them up and their households, and all the men that appertained unto Korah, and all their goods" (Num. 16:32).

The other example of a decisive and challenging No in the Bible is found much later, possibly six hundred years after the event just mentioned. Nehemiah, who had given up a high and honorable post at the court of the King of Persia in order to direct the rebuilding of the walls of

Jerusalem and the Temple and the whole structure of the second Commonwealth after the Babylonian exile, was being hindered by those who did not want this distinctive religious and social life of the Jews to be rebuilt. These hostile forces induced Sanballat, the Persian governor of the district, to stop the work on the walls and the Temple, and Sanballat ordered Nehemiah to meet him at the plain of Ono. To this Nehemiah, as we learn in his book (Neh. 6:3) gave the great refusal, the historic No: "I am doing a great work, so that I cannot come down" (*M'locho g'do-lo ani oseh, v'lo uchal lore-des*). He would not be beguiled by any side issue from his great mission. He continued at this great work, and the Temple and city walls and the new Commonwealth were rebuilt and organized — and Judaism lived on.

Shall we not spend a moment comparing these two refusals, even as we compared the Czar's and Dollfuss'? One group — the Korah class — refuses to *go up*, the other group with Nehemiah at their head refuses to *go down;* they *will* stay *up*. Staying up and refusing to go up are two ways of viewing life and its opportunities and obligations. The two attitudes turn about the one question of Idealism. Idealism has had a hard time of it in the twentieth century. The spirit of cynicism is abroad, that nothing amounts to much anyhow. The attitude of *nil admirari* — to admire nothing — to be lukewarm on everything, to have no consuming convictions, to recognize no flaming banners — that attitude has become quite popular, and every other attitude is laughed at as *Schwaermerei* — pure frothing — and as a sign of immaturity of thought. All sentiment is discouraged as sentimentality, all loyalty as fanaticism. There are no mountains of decision, no eternal sanctions, no everlasting prohibitions.

In step with this pedestrian and deflated social outlook has come the resultant deterioration of our human values.

The attitude of Korah and his band has been dominant. The refusal of which he was guilty, how often is it our refusal! We will not go up, we won't try the high ground, we believe only in low aims and that human nature is depraved and that it is sodden and that it cannot rise on the tides of the spirit to anything that is inspiring. We prefer to remain down here. Folks call it keeping their feet on the ground. It is really keeping themselves prisoners to little petty things and refusing to be liberated to the heights. We prefer to keep our feet on the ground — producing a lot of grumblers and small critics and little else — a dreamless and a soulless band who contribute nothing to life but its creak and its croaking. Part of the product of that spirit is seen in much of the life about us, in much of the literature in our magazines, and in much of the drama on the stage and the movies. Keeping their feet on the ground means to many people getting deeper and deeper into the mire and the dirt and the slough of hopeless despond.

The other group — for there is another group even in this third decade of the twentieth century who will not bow to Baal — has the Nehemiah spirit and attitude and will take the high plane, the higher view, the ideals and idealism which mean something in our life. We refuse, say these, to be destroyed and blinded in the plain of Ono where the cynic prevails — where there is no flaming banner, no terrific impulse toward the heights. We are doing a great work and we can't go down, we will not debase ourselves, we *will not stoop to conquer.* These people believe in their job, that it is worth while, that they are engaged in a great work, a building project for mankind, a life's aim with an architect's drawing to realize in a mansion of the soul. These Nehemiah people believe in moral tension (instead of moral looseness based on the contention that nothing counts anyhow). They believe in keeping tuned up. They can't let down. They have ideals, they are going to keep their flag flying. They have before them the vision of the permanent horizon, which Ludwig Lewisohn has so eloquently presented in his latest book.

Young people, especially you students of the high schools who recently received your January diplomas, may I say this to you: You obtained much from your studies, here and there the inspiration of some stimulating teachers. But there are two things without which you will depart utterly poor from the rich feast of your school life. One is a great friendship — perhaps it can only be one great attachment which you have made and which can be so called. And the other is the acceptance of the value of ideals above all else. If you take these ideals as your heritage, your guiding force as you go out into the world to take up your chosen tasks, you will be clad as it were in shining armor. Nothing will sully you; you will go out with a new hope because of your idealism. You will carry your banners high, compromise them never. The world of Sanballats may come to you and invite you into the soggy plains of Ono, but realizing that you are engaged in a great work, you will say, "I cannot come down." You will be challenged every day — sometimes every hour — by someone calling, "Come down, leave your work, abandon this high moral tension, be yourself, give your instincts a chance, drop your medieval self-restraint — don't sacrifice yourself through any Messiah-complex, come down into the comfortable valley of Ono, life is short at the best, eat and be merry while you may and let dreams go hang. Come down here into the plain of Ono where each is on his own, and goes a-rooting for his own, on the lowest plane with no obligation to any code higher than that of self-preservation. Come down here, you don't see the stars here, but also you aren't tempted to crane and cramp your neck. Come down, it's rather un-spectacular, but it has no great peril of adventures and you can always have a pretty full stomach. Come down and forget the heights."

On the other hand, you'll hear the high challenge, "Come up, come up, out of the noise and the muck where you lose your sense of proportion and your soul. Come up out of the crush for self-advantage, where sweat and tears and blood are all around. Come up where the clear stars shine and the voice of God is heard, and where one can reach out toward the divine even though his feet are on the ground. Come up where the splendor of honor and duty and sacrifice and service strikes full upon our senses."

From day to day we are thus besieged. Let us not say No like Dathan and Abiram who would not go up, who preferred their low and false and apparent horizons, who were so fearful of being deceived by sentiment that they closed their eyes to every sunlit glory and saw only its shadow — and thought they saw reality. These will not go up, and they lose the world and themselves. Their No is decisive for a lost opportunity, a frustrated and defeated life.

But again, too, we are besieged by others who call to us, "Come down into the Valley of Ono," where there are no dreams and there is no glow. Come down to what folks call real life. Answer them, yes, real life; it is up here where I have a great task to perform. I can't come down. Here, too, the No is decisive. It means a full, throbbing, meaningful, complete life. It means that we are building the walls of a new Jerusalem, as Nehemiah built. We are raising aloft the Temple of the Most High. To those who beckon us to come down, let us answer the Everlasting No!

THE FLOOD, DOVE, AND RAINBOW —
AND ANOTHER BYSTANDER

THE EARLY CHAPTERS of the Book of Genesis were read recently as Scriptural portions in the synagogue. If you wish, the stories they tell may be taken literally, but as for me I find them filled with suggestions that should be helpful for our thinking in this day of ours. The Flood and the Tower of Babel, Noah and the Ark, the Raven and the Dove and the Rainbow — and an imaginary bystander — all these are the scenery and the dramatis personae of the present age. Let us take them up, one by one.

Noah is saved because "he walked with God." He was not of that group, whom we may call the "one-day pious," who sing of the God of love and pray to the God of mercy, and bow down to the Father who is in heaven — and then go forth and organize hate groups and spread calumnies against some of the children of that Father to whom they prayed — if you can call that praying. It is said of Noah that he was "in his generation a righteous man" — not a self-conscious saint, perfection personified, as unattractive as it is unreal, but a rather average man, considered good in a generation of violence. His saving grace — the grace that saved him — was that "Noah walked with God," and that he built his ark for flood times. He did not wait for the waters to overwhelm him or even to threaten his safety, but walking with God — keeping his daily tryst with Him, keeping spiritually fit by spiritual exercise, fortifying himself not only by frequent orisons but by living his daily life within sight and reach of the divine — he had built his ark of safety against

October 21, 1945.

all the floods of earthly happenings; to which ark, buoyant above the raging floods, he might repair and preserve that serenity and faith and calm trust in God which so many of us lose in our daily flight from godly companionship.

Then came the Flood, as it came to this generation of man, to this *dor hammabbul*, this flood generation, because "the earth was corrupt before God," and therefore "the earth was filled with violence." That violence did not only come *after* the flood, but had prevailed before it, through the corruption that had spread through the earth. The flood of violence is here on the earth these days, the flood of starvation and of wounds and of death — and the postwar confusion and distrust — because of the precedent corruption and violence of which all of us, all nations in this *dor hammabbul*, were guilty. And in this catastrophe, this convulsion of civilization, we ask ourselves as did the people of Noah's time, does this mean the end of the earth, does this mean another dark age, is this just the forerunner of more violence and chaos and suffering; or does it bring some hope of better things to come?

As in the Bible story different answers are made to all these anxious self-questionings by the many kinds of bystanders, symbolized in the ancient tale by strange dramatis personae. There is first the Raven, dark in color, darker in the foreboding and the terror it brings. The Raven is sent out to reconnoiter and soon comes back — reporting that the flood continues and there is no dry spot on earth, nothing to suggest that normal and decent and gracious living is anywhere in sight. Nevermore! says the Raven. The future, says the Raven, is as black as the past. Yes, the Raven declares, the floods which buoy up your ark will eventually disappear — but think of the mud left behind, think of the destruction that has been wrought, the very texture of your economy torn apart. Evil days and terrorizing nights will still be your lot for a very long time. Perhaps order and the peace will come: Nevermore!

The same croaking voice is heard today. The pessimist is with us with cries of revolution and evil hiding underground, soon to rise again to trouble this wrecked and wretched earth. With all his croaking the pessimist is needed, and is definitely helpful, if he does not induce a paralyzing fear. Let the pessimist warn us not to lose our alertness, not to let up too soon, not to become sentimentally too soft in our treatment of those who shot up our world and spread abroad the long-planned and carefully and meticulously woven net of violence and hate and destruction into which our trusting and lazy natures had been lured. Let us watch the kind of peace that is made — keeping the pessimist's gloomy picture of deadly despair and revived horror before us. Let us do all we can to destroy the germs of hate and intolerance — the oozing mud which the pessimist is sure will remain to keep us bogged down indefinitely and do the work which Hitler could not do with all his military machine, the oozing mud of intolerance and hate and hatemongers — but let us not give over to despair with the cry "Nevermore." The pessimist is useful in pricking us into constant alertness and watchfulness — but let him not clip the wings of our hope of world betterment.

But after the Raven went forth the Dove to make another survey of the raging floodwaters. After a rather hasty examination, she — the Dove is *Yonah* in the Hebrew language, feminine in gender — came swinging back to the Ark with a freshly plucked olive leaf in her mouth. See, she said, the tops of the olive trees are visible as you may note from the leaf I bring you, and the flood will soon disappear and all will soon be normal. Peace is just around the corner — and order and rehabilitation; all the refuse will be swept up and before you know it we will be as we were before. Yes, even better, says the Dove, for the earth will have been cleansed of all noisome things by the devastating but cleansing waters. That Dove is a symbol of the quick and easy optimist, who today is saying the same things in practically the same words. The tops of the olive trees are visible, here is the olive leaf, and before you know it we will all be living in peace together — and there will be no more hate and no more ruthlessness and no more Nazis on the prowl and no more Japanese war lords to kill and maim and destroy. The dove is a nice bird, and coos so innocently and "as gently as any sucking dove" — but she doesn't see very far nor examine very carefully all parts of the scene — she just looks for a bit of olive leaf. Guard against being lulled to sleep into a dream of swift and easy peace by these well-intentioned optimists, who seem never to read history, and seldom to realize that evil often goes underground when it must, to reappear when it can. The dovelike optimist may be a good sedative for temporary use — but beware of being made a slave to its poppy and mandragora.

Then comes God and points to His covenant in the sky — "the bow in the clouds" — the rainbow which lights up not only one little spot, which doesn't shine in pure white light, but which bends across the whole sky in a long, long trail of mixed colors. That is the symbol of the safe and sane optimist who knows that white light in all its purity is not with us mortals, but with God alone, that many and varied motives and needs and impulses make up the vast human approach toward the destruction of evil and the building of the mansion of a better world. This rainbow covenant of God with man symbolizes the long-range optimist, who doesn't expect the olive leaf's appearance to hush all the brutish noises of the world, who doesn't lose faith in God and man because we cannot and do not ascend the mountain of the Lord in one Brobdingnagian step. The first step toward the world of peace that is lasting and righteous must be taken as soon as possible, without any delay that may give time and opportunity for the waters of disunity to come in again; the world organization on wise lines must be not only signed, as it was last week, but put to work. There must be a return to that Noachic "walking with God" and building an ark against a third coming of the flood of world catastrophe in this century — perhaps in this half-century. But let it all be based and predicated on the long-range view — the wise and careful and plodding, yet at the same time the visionful and winged yet slower and surer optimism which knows that not one step but many lead up to the altar of peace. With the coming of the atomic bomb, which cannot long be kept a secret of the United States or one or two more nations, there is an imperative demand for a strong United Nations organization now!

There is yet one bystander of the flood who isn't mentioned in the Bible account but who I am certain must have been there, as he is always with us. That bystander is the nonchalant person who with a wave of the hand brushes aside Raven and Dove, and closes his eyes on the Rainbow — and who with a spacious gesture of omniscience announces that Raven and Dove and Rainbow are a bit of histrionics and mean nothing, that Flood follows Flood, when confusion of tongues and Towers of Babel do not, that neither optimist — swift or slow — nor pessimist, dark and foreboding, tells the true story, for there is no plan nor hope in the world — that the story of the universe and of man in it is but "a tale told by an idiot, full of sound and fury, signifying nothing." There are some of our writers of today and yesterday who do not recognize any moral order in the world, who scoff at heroism and dismiss anything that savors of loftiness and sublimity as sheer nonsense. Says one character in Arthur Koestler's book *Arrival and Departure:*

What after all is courage? A matter of glands, nerves, patterns of reaction conditioned by heredity and early experiences. A drop of iodine less in the thyroid, a sadistic governess or an over-affectionate aunt, a slight variation in the electric resistance of the medullary ganglions, and the hero becomes a coward, the patriot becomes a traitor. Touched with the magic rod of cause and effect, the actions of men are emptied of their so-called moral content.

That bystander in the drama of the Flood is the cynic who laughs at heroism and courage and love and dreams and hope of a decent, civilized world after the floodwaters recede. He sees only frustration, other floods, and at best confusion of tongues and a Tower of Babel. He never sees God, above it all; and so he is dreadfully afraid — always afraid — afraid of the dark! Let us guard against the cynicism of those who deny the moral content of human actions; who sneer at God's rainbow covenant; who scoff at progress and plan; who deride those who dream of fashioning dykes to hold back the flood waters in the years to come; who insist that you can't wipe out hate in the world, or intolerance, or wars; who admit that the lights go on now and then in the habitations of humanity only to go out again, and soon; and who suggest only that we cower in the darkness they have evoked. Rather let us pay heed to the Raven that warns — and to the Dove which waves the olive leaf — and above all to the Rainbow which tells that God's covenant of peace is there, for that long, long effort of His children to destroy the corruption and violence which stand in the way of human happiness and world peace.

217

TWO VOICES — TO WHICH SHALL WE LISTEN?

Two voices there are; one of the sea,
One of the mountains; each a mighty voice.
Wordsworth.

WHEN THE SHADOWS of this evening have drawn their curtains over the flaming western sky, and night tiptoes over the mountains, and stars bejewel the domed sky, then enters the holiest day of the Jewish year. Usually we call the Yom Kippur the Sabbath of Sabbaths, but in this year 5703, Atonement Day brings a message this world sorely needs more than in years past. It finds Israel today, as all through the centuries, peculiarly receptive to its message, even though it announces hard truths and points minatory finger as does no other holy day. It is pre-eminently the one day when Israel's soul speaks in terms of eternity. A voice as from on high calls, "Return, Atone!" That demand is insistent and clearly audible as at no other time of the year. We pray that Israel will answer: "This is the generation that seeks Thee." And the assurance comes from on high: "If only thou diligently hearken unto the voice ... the Lord thy God will bless thee" (Deut. 15: 5, 6).

The voice: "Hearken unto the voice," is the command. But which of the many voices is "the voice"? In our ears at least two voices claim attention — not just one. The poet, Wordsworth, noted this and he discerned the voice of the sea and the voice of the mountains. Each speaks to a different mood in man. So, too, noted the writer of that vivid narrative of the prophet Elijah when Jezebel had put the true prophets to the sword. He wanted to hear

---

September 20, 1942.

the voice of the Lord assuring him that, though he was now cowering in a cave, the final victory would be Elijah's and God's and not Jezebel's. He was waiting for a voice, *the* voice. God told Elijah to "stand on the mount before the Lord," there to listen for God's voice. But two sets of voices were heard, one of a great and strong wind that rent the mountains, of a terrible earthquake, and of a fire — but Elijah knew the Lord was not in them, that was not God's voice. After all these phenomena of violent nature came "a still small voice" *(kol demomoh dakkeh)*. Elijah immediately knew that God was in that still small voice — nay, He *was* the still small voice. You see, there are two voices with two moods — even as there were the voice of Jacob and the hands of Esau — two contrasting natures of the human soul. They represent man's immemorial battle with himself; his earth and sky, his dust and star, perpetually warring with each other. Which shall be victorious — to which shall we give heed? Surely only one voice calls to us on the Kol Nidre — to one voice alone shall we listen. It is the *kol kore bamidbar* — the voice calling in the wilderness of today.

But to be able to turn a deaf ear to the strident voice and listen solely to the still small voice, we must appraise both of them. We must come to know them for what they are. Sometimes they both sound so plausible that we must test them now under conditions which only this holy day offers. There is first the voice of the wind, of the earthquake, and of the fire — all destructive and cruel — the voice that is hard and hairy like the hand of Esau, the wild man. The voice of the sea, turbulent, fitful and fickle, now smooth as silk in its promises and propaganda and soon like a furious beast gnashing its teeth as the phosphorescent waves run high. The voice of the sea, moaning, complaining for *weltraum*, when not arrogant and threatening, treacherous; never at rest and always changing, never steady, never stable — unpredictable, the voice of evil in the world. That voice so often speaks to you and me. Let us appraise it for what it is, and close our ears to it.

The sea voice, the wind voice, the earthquake and fire voice — hear now the words it speaks. It says to you and me, "Stand for yourself alone, be the arch-isolationist, make the gospel of selfishness your Bible, and forget all those weakly foolish admonitions about charity and kindness and mercy. Be unrelenting and cruel and ruthless, for that way achieves for you the earth and the fulness thereof." It sneeringly demands of us that we hold in contempt all those things that we prided ourselves were the truest ideals and surest goals of human striving. When from the pulpit we are urged to wish for the right New Year's gift to us — not money, not riches, not wealth, but an understanding heart, there rises in protest in many of us the sea voice, the voice of the cynic, who has lost all sight of ideals if ever he had glimpsed them; the voice of the materialist, who only values that which enriches his personal self; the voice of the realist, as he proudly calls himself, who has no vision of those things that his eyes cannot see, and whispers, "No, no — I wish for gold and power — for myself and mine." As though gold and power could buy health and friends and the thrills of love and all that means true happiness!

It is the voice of the sea — the wanton raucous sea — which we have heard to our disgust over the short-wave radio, and which seeks to engulf all things and our very personalities in it, and make us over into the unrelenting, fickle, cruel thing which it is — not human but brutal and of the beast. That voice speaks to us so attractively throughout the year — so demandingly and insistently — holding before our eyes the luscious apple of temptation that means subjugation to our appetites, and bending the knee to nothing else but gold and physical pleasure and the lust for power. It is the voice abroad today in Europe, with Germany and Italy and its lickspittles and its trumpeters, and soon — mayhap for a long time — there will be no other voice than that. Surely we will not listen to it. Shutting our ears to it here, we may yet in a world gone mad keep our America and the democracies, at least, islands of sanity; we may make sure that they will fight triumphantly to preserve and cherish the heritage of the centuries and sustain the spirit of man. Let us shut our ears to the voice of the cynic, the materialist, the so-called realist — who in fact worships nothing but the god of self and of the main chance, and mayhap we, our America, the United Nations, and gradually the other nations may be redeemed of the horror which like a pestilence has spread over the world. Let us shut our ears to the voice of the sea! Otherwise we are treasonable to our Jewish faith, to American and world democracy, and to human decency.

In its stead comes the voice of the mountains, the voice that dominates this holiest of days. Listen to it, for it is indeed "celestial melody." It is steadying, for it says: "Have faith in goodness and in justice and in truth and in mercy even though the mountains fall, even though now so much that we cherished has crumbled to the earth." The voice of the mountain is deliberate and cool and reassuring, holding something ethereal in it as though it had come from recent communion with the angels, sounding like the long-silenced — yet dimly remembered — voice of a saintly father or mother, appealing even while warning. It is the voice of conscience regnant on this Yom Kippur Day.

How the world needs that voice today! As men turned increasingly deaf ears to it, the woes of the world have multiplied, until we are now seeing a reversion to barbarism and godlessness, the coming in of a tide of evil that threatens to inundate the fields of righteousness and godliness and human freedom which have been so sedulously cultivated throughout the agelong past of mankind. The voice of the mountains, the still small voice of religion and of faith, the authentic voice of Kol Nidre appeals to us now: It says, "Don't listen to that other voice so popular in many quarters that wants you to forget God, to be a pagan and a cynic, sneering even at the Holy of Holies." The still small voice! Listen to *it*, as it brings to us the cry of the millions of Israel who have been caught in the returning and devastating tide of barbarism; listen to the pain of all brothers and sisters who have upheld their faith even though the forces of evil rage and bluster and destroy. Be of good faith, and trust in the final outcome of the right, and hold fast and be resolute until victory comes, a victory that will be worth while and will justify all the sacrifice only if we preserve the faith in those things which the still small voice whispers.

The old parable about the Days of Awe — the New Year and the Day of Atonement — properly understood is not a mere fable for children but has its sound core of truth for you and me. The parable held that God sits in His celestial abode above the expanse of the blue heavens, before the Book of Life, and on the Rosh Hashonah He writes down each human being's destiny for the New Year, *Mi Yichye, Mi Yomus,* who will live and who will die; and on the Day of Atonement God seals that record and it stands as inscribed. The New Year came ten days ago — and we made our resolutions, we offered our prayers and uttered our wishes, and *"we listened to the voice."* That was a good beginning and all was auspicious that the recording for a happy and good year would stand. If we tonight and throughout the Atonement Day fulfil the obligations of the holiest of days, if we atone — as we as Jews, as all America, the appeasing democracies and other nations must — and make restitution and *continue to listen to this still small voice,* shutting our ears to the vicious other voice — the voice of cynicism, unfaith, Fascism, Nazism, and ruthless cruelty — then God will place His final seal upon the record for a Good Year. The recording — and the sealing — is after all in our own hands, according to the parable. As *we* resolve, as *we* utter our heart's wishes, as *we* atone and humble our hearts before God, we place on record in the Book of Life our destiny — as *we* listen to one voice or the other we seal that destiny for good or for evil. Not only is that true of men, but also of nations. Out of the Book of Deuteronomy comes the assurance, "If only thou wilt hearken to the voice" *(Rak im shomoah tishma bakkol — adonoy elocheche bayrach'cho),* "the Lord thy God will bless thee." It is written of the Atonement Eve, Kol Nidre — which is this evening:

> Comes the witching hour of night,
> Orbed in the moon and bright,
> And the stars they glisten, glisten,
> Seeming with bright eyes to listen —
> For what listen they? The still small voice,
> That never rests, as it points to our choice.

For what may we listen — now and through the year? For the voice of the mountains, the voice of conscience, the voice of faith, the still small voice — God's voice that warns, that speaks in love to all His children, the voice which now assures us: *"Solachti,* I have pardoned," and you shall be sealed for a Happy New Year.

THE SUBMERGED CATHEDRAL

A LEGEND current in Britanny tells of a wonderful Cathedral at Lyonesse, hard by the sea, which was the pride of all the people of that section of France. It had been erected not in one year or generation, but through over a hundred years, each generation adding something with the funds it had gathered with much sacrifice — the foundation here, the pillars there, an arch or a nave — while artists for over a century vied with each other in producing lovingly the statues of saints for the many niches in the growing structure. Finally the Cathedral in all its loveliness was completed, and in it the people of Lyonesse offered their orisons and found strength and comfort in their hard and bare life. And so it stood for many years, until a stranger knight schemed its destruction and for that purpose wooed a wilful princess of the neighborhood and obtained from her the key to turn the valve to let in the waters of the sea. So the Cathedral was submerged beneath the briny waters, and at the edge of the lake thus formed the devout people would stand vigil and offer their prayers while they saw beneath the water the implacable waves pounding and battering the great pillars and the salt water making deep gashes in the heavy foundation stones. But because of those faithful prayers and never-ceasing vigils, there came a time when the waters subsided and the submerged Cathedral rose again to the light of day and its bells again sounded the call for worship.

Today in many lands the legend of Lyonesse and the submerged Cathedral has become the everyday truth and fact. The Cathedral of the spirit, the Cathedral of faith, the Cathedral of human rights has been dismally and tragically engulfed by negation and arrogance in nations and in individual lives, while much that is fine and lovely and of good report has been corroded by surviving ancient savagery and renewed and improved modern forms of old-time hates, prejudices, and selfishness. Only faintly do the bells of faith and decency and honor sound from the depths, while all that conduced to strength amid life's struggle, all that gave courage and comfort when adversity pressed upon the souls of men, all life's graciousness, all that nourished the power of self-control and moral erectness and spiritual grandeur is utterly submerged. Will the Cathedral rise again to bless the human race? Only if vigils again are kept by the faithful, and solemn prayers again ascend from humble hearts will that Cathedral rise again to give of its radiance to human life.

Let us look at the modern submerged Cathedral, and ask what caused the tragic situation in which the world finds itself today. There are five great columns — monoliths of righteousness — that have been slowly fashioned in the course of the ages to sustain the weight and lofty naves of the Cathedral of humanity, and it is because the waters of evil have sadly corroded these pillars that the chaos and suffering and horror of the present hour infest our daily lives. The ancient sage, Simon the Just, spoke of three such pillars, upon which the world rests, *Torah* or moral teaching, *Abodah* or worship and reverence, and *Gemilut Hasodim* or kindliness, human brotherhood. There are also other pillars, supplemental to these and necessary in our greatly complex age, which have crumbled before our eyes and have brought down upon our generation its submerged Cathedral. Men have perverted the right and have enthroned their pride and their arrogance and have forgotten reverence and honor and decency and brotherhood.

General indictments of the age will not get us very far.

Had we not better try to discover just what gave way in the Cathedral of humanity that brought about this submergence of all that we hold dear? Well, it seems to me that *Torah* — the first great column which the teacher of old referred to — *moral teaching, moral stamina* — has been undermined both in individuals and in nations. While it is true that treaties between nations were torn up and disregarded in the ages past, never before has this been done so frequently and so nonchalantly as in the past twenty or thirty years. Something must have happened within the conscience and character of men and nations long before to have brought about this cavalier disregard of the given word and subscribed name. It may be that this resulted from the theory of the Superman which Nietzsche promulgated at the end of the last century: that nothing must stand in the way of the Superman's ambitions, his plans — no considerations of honor, of truth, or of justice or common decency — the only demand on him being that he grasp and hold whatever he desires. Of course, such a theory could not be considered unless at first there had come a loosening of the belief in a Holy God, a God of righteousness. The briny waves of disbelief and negation and skepticism and cynicism and atheism had already corroded that strong column — and it gave way in our twentieth century, and in that immoral way the enemies of society, of the Communist and Fascist and Nazi stripe, hewed their path to power. *One pillar broke down!* And the most truculent of the nations, Germany, Italy, Japan, and Russia, unscrupulously grasped the smaller nations and made them subservient.

The second pillar of the Cathedral has fared equally ill. *Abodah*, the recognition of God in the life of each of us and of the nations, reverence for Him and His law, and seeing in every human being the spark of the divine and the inherent human rights that go with it — all this has been seriously weakened in the society of men and nations. Science, in the exhilaration of its tremendous discoveries and vast accomplishments, induced many people — the lesser pseudo scientists — to believe that the veil of mystery of life had been rent asunder, or promised to be soon. And with this belief went the presumption that nothing existed in the world or the heart of man that could not some day be perceived by the means that science had at its disposal; that all that is in the world is only material and can be explained by the various laws that science has evolved; that there is nothing in all the world and in the heart of man but hydrogen and oxygen and a few other composites which would explain all the universe and life itself. The secular age dawned with skepticism and atheism following in its train and the pagan view of life replacing the old Hebraic teaching of holiness and godliness and reverence. And so the second pillar gradually crumbled! And men and nations ran riot worshiping any sort of golden calf of power, lust, or selfish greed their hearts desired.

The third pillar in the Cathedral of the good and the true went out the same way. They called it of old *Gemilut Hasodim,* kindliness, mercy, brotherliness. The most attractive and blessed emotion of man, the gentlest pulsation of the human heart became contemptible in the eyes of many, as something purely sentimental and as a definite sign of weakness in men and nations. It was replaced by hate and hardness, by unbelievable cruelty of man toward his fellow-man. The climax in this tragedy of submergence of loving-kindness can be found in the horror tales that come out of the Nazi concentration camps, in the implacable persecution of groups, Christian and Jewish, which will not — cannot — bow down to this new swastika idol of malevolence and sadism. And so this

227

third pillar went out with the tide of hate and horror! And Pastor Hall in the films becomes the solemn indictment of a nation crazed into terrorism, though it is a mere drop in the ocean of tears from the eyes and hearts of many millions of the children of men.

Yet, beside the corroded pillars which have been mentioned there are others in the Cathedral of humanity which are clearly breaking down — yielding in many lands. They are, of course, only replicas of the pillars which Simon the Just enumerated, representing the modern political manifestations and reproductions of *Torah, Abodah,* and *Gemilut Hasodim.* And they are the columns which are very dear to us Americans in that they support the noble architrave and dome of democracy. We might call these pillars truth, justice, and inherent human rights, to which our Republic is dedicated. How ruthlessly have the waters of the dictators battered these pillars! Truth is disregarded, and propagandists of the totalitarians are urged to tell lies often and boldly, for they are told that the sinister fabrications will be believed because oft repeated and brazenly announced. Machiavelli was a tyro in the use of political deception compared to these modern monsters of untruth. Thus into this country there has flowed an ever increasing stream of lying propaganda seeking to destroy our American unity and to set up barriers between citizen and citizen — and thus to divide and conquer. Justice in the gates has become despised in those dictator lands, and in the courts of those countries the dictum rules that only that which is favorable to the partisan cause of naziism is to have weight and be the deciding factor.

The reverence for human rights inherent in man as a child of God has been one of the first things we find discarded in the new order of totalitarian politics. What we in America consider fundamental in government and pri-

vate relations, conducing to decency and human welfare
as well as peace within our borders, is sneered at and
thrown aside by the Stalins and Mussolinis and Hitlers.
They have no use for the human rights to life, liberty,
and the pursuit of happiness, for the freedom of speech,
of the press, of peaceful assembly and of worship — the
right of conscience and religion. It is these pillars of the
Cathedral at which they have most savagely slashed and
aimed their sledge-hammer blows. Is it any wonder that
these columns have given way in the totalitarian lands?
One after another of these pillars has been weakened —
hence the submergence of the Cathedral, there in those
lands.

Two considerations arise from the contemplation of
what happened to the Cathedral in those unhappy countries and the misery that has been inflicted thereby on
many innocent people and nations. One is that once the
alien knight woos the *wilful princess* and turns the valve
which lets in the waters, submerging the Cathedral in one
land, the peril of a similar submergence comes to other
lands. The evil spreads! Once the waters are let in, it is
almost impossible to keep them from spreading far and
wide. One can't isolate one's self — or one's nation — from
the devastating flood. There are always alien knights of
evil and wilful princesses, fifth column agitators, who
make it their business to have the submerging waters
seep into other lands.

The second consideration is that no such vast revolution, no such successful attack on the pillars of the Cathedral of humanity, could have been successful, if there had
not been a very considerable weakening of the foundations of those columns long before — a weakening in the
fundamentals of honor, justice, reverence, religious devotion generally in human society. The pagan and the secular view of life as opposed to the Hebraic-Christian view

of righteousness and holiness and the moral order of the universe must have grown up as a noxious weed in the world at large. All social, religious, and political groups and the individuals that compose them must have been touched by the plague, before it could be possible for economic disaster and the presence of unscrupulous demagogues to crystallize it into the horrible monster of evil that has shot up the world. Each social group, each religious organization, each individual — you and I — must have been developing within itself some indifference to the things of the spirit, some touch of materialism, some unbelief which lent virulence to the plague when it finally broke out. We are all to blame for the Hitlers and the Mussolinis and the Stalins, for we have prepared a fertile soil for the noxious seed of hate and horror, of pagan unbelief and arrogant lust of power.

And what did the men and women of Lyonesse do when their beloved Cathedral was submerged? The legend tells us that they kept vigil, listening to the faint sound of the bell tolling beneath the waves, and that they lifted their hearts in daily orisons supplicating that the Cathedral might rise again. That is our task, that must be our program — *vigil* and *worship* — watchful alertness for the pillars of the Cathedral in our midst which, thank God, still stand, so that with eyes open we may seek out any alien knight and wilful person who may endanger our Cathedral. We must participate in those exercises of our religion that shall keep alive within us the sense of God's nearness and the urgency of His law upon us, that shall preserve our spiritual values and control our passions and lusts and keep us humble and faithful servants of our fellow-men and of the Most High. Thus we can direct the so-called wave of the future and preserve our precious heritage — represented by the five pillars of the Temple of Righteousness. Then the waters of evil will subside and the submerged Cathedral will again rise to bless all the nations of the earth.

WHY I AM A JEW

I AM HAPPY to participate in this forum of religion, but not because I am at all desirous of presenting an apologia for my own beliefs or for those of the Jewish people generally. For I believe that such an apologia, to be trustworthy and dependable, cannot be one of words; it must be found in life alone, in the translation of belief into conduct. What effect a man's or a people's religious beliefs have had on his or their way of life is the yardstick of appraisal; therein is the surest, strongest, and most convincing apologia for one's credo.

What makes this a happy participation on my part is that a symposium such as this is indicative of the coming into the world of saner standards of thought and judgment, of truly civilized attitudes and modes of approach, of humility in the face of a complex world and its strange script, a spirit of toleration and willingness to know and to understand, without any compulsion to conversion or change. I am glad to be a party to this symposium because it is an intellectual and spiritual venture truly sanctified, because it is far removed from that ugly, uncivilized — certainly un-Jewish and un-Christian — impulse to cry down fanatically every belief that happens not to be ours; because it evinces a desire to know the basis of men's faith, to understand and to assay and test men's beliefs through knowledge rather than through unreliable hearsay or age-old, grimy prejudice. Such a program as this symposium on religion is another plank laid down on that high bridge which will eventually span the dread chasm of religious separateness, suspicion, and hostility, and bring peace and charity and good will into that one field where they should always have grown naturally.

Instead of telling you item by item why I am a Jew, I should have preferred to proceed as Nathan the Wise did, according to the drama of Lessing, when the Sultan held a similar symposium in the dim past. A Christian and a Mohammedan had laid down before the Sultan and his assembled court the excellencies of their respective beliefs; and then it came to Nathan the Wise to tell why he was a Jew. Instead he asked the Sultan's permission to tell the story of the Three Rings. It was as follows: In a certain family there had been handed down from father to son from time immemorial a ring which, it was understood by the family tradition, possessed the power of bringing happiness and righteousness, honor and reverence and truth to the one who wore it. Each father successively handed it down at his dying hour to the son he loved best. There came a time when the father who had possession of the ring had three sons for whom he bore an equal love. To whom should he give the precious ring? He called a goldsmith and had him make two other rings exactly like the true one, and at his dying hour he called to his bedside separately each of the three sons and, telling him the exceptional virtues of the ring, presented it to him.

After the days of mourning had passed the sons noted the ring on each other's fingers and each told the same story of how he came into the possession of it, told of its virtues and insisted that he and he alone had the genuine ring. The three quarreled and in the end repaired to a great and wise judge. He heard their story and commented: "Is it not true that your father told you that the genuine ring had the magic virtue of beautifying and ennobling the life of the one who possessed it?" They agreed that it was so. Said the judge: "Then only time can tell who has the genuine ring. Wait a thousand, thousand years, and come before the wise judge of those days and state your case, and he will be able to determine by the life you have lived, by the dreams you dreamed, the visions you saw and the works you accomplished, which of you has the genuine ring." And thus — Nathan the Wise ended. I should have liked to end here — but I have been requested to tell why I am a Jew.

So I pass beyond the point made by Nathan the Wise. But when I answer the question why I am a Jew, you may be sure that it is with no desire or ambition to convert any hearer to my faith, for you may take for granted that I feel certain that for you your faith is as good as mine is for me. Neither is there any intention on my part to unfurl my religious banner in any bragging, chauvinistic sense, for I am rather humble on the whole matter of Pilate's old question: What is truth? All I say is that to me, with my heart, my mind, my forebears, my traditions, my racial heritage, that which we call Judaism appeals as the truth. It is the truth from the place where I stand; yours is the truth from the place where you stand. And that is all we know of the truth.

Why am I a Jew? Of course, as every one of you has already guessed, I am a Jew because I was born a Jew, was suckled at the breast of a pious Jewish mother, and was taught at her knees my Jewish prayers to the God of Israel. I am a Jew because in the formative years of my childhood, which are so determining, I lived in the midst of a Jewish community. But there is more in that birthmark of Judaism than appears on the surface. The racial experience, the group experience, the happenings of the family through the ages both physically and spiritually are ineradicable. They inevitably leave their residuum, their deposit, in the physical and mental composition of each later generation. There is something in the physical deposit of the race or group which keeps it immune from certain diseases and makes it hospitable to others. So there is something in the spiritual, the intellectual, the emotional deposit which makes it hostile or hospitable to certain ideas and outlooks. I am a Jew because that spiritual residuum, being of the Jewish kind, makes me agreeable, hospitable, to the attitudes, the concepts, the outlook, the dreams and beliefs, the hopes and ideas, the accent of creed which is Jewish.

So that through birth and therefore emotionally, perhaps you might also say instinctively, the Jewish religion appeals to me. It is my accent of thought and feeling because of the ages that are back of me and out of which I came. But naturally no reasoning person, when intellectual maturity arrives, or even at the earlier age when reason asserts itself, is willing to abide by that instinct, that purely passive group-survival, in a field so important as that which concerns our relationship to the universe and to God. So there came a period when I asked myself: Are these Jewish beliefs that came to me through the heritage of the ages valid before the throne of reason?

In judging for myself that validity I called to my aid all the truth that has come to me from the various fields of knowledge, from the science that brings report of the external world and from the science that tells of the psychic, the inner cosmos of the human soul. I did not say, here is my faith, revealed long ago to my people by our Heavenly Father, and it must stand in a compartment of my intellectual treasury by itself, and I have no right to test it as I try to test all other concepts. No, I took up the concepts of my Jewish faith to test them by all the knowledge that is part of the continuous revelation of God given to us in each age and so bountifully especially in our own. And then, once I was sure that I was handling truth in this later revelation of science, no matter if it came from the lens of telescope or microscope, or through the close reasoning of disciplined and well-trained minds, or through the intuitions and inexplicable insights of the poet, the seer, and the prophet — whether he lived two or three thousand years ago or sang to us but yesterday — I was ready to cancel, to strike out or to substitute for that instinctive belief that came to me because I derived from the seed of Abraham.

And thus tested before the bar of reason my Jewish beliefs are still possessed of their ancient validity for me — and more, very much more are they corroborated. Science of today agrees, as Professor Jeans says, that the universe begins to look like "a great thought," and that "a great architect of the universe" does exist. To the question that arises like a cry from the human heart, "What is it all about?" science of today answers, as does Professor Eddington, not that it is only about atoms and chaos — a universe of fiery globes, moving to an impending doom — but "rather it is about a spirit in which truth has its shrine, with potentialities of self-fulfilment in its responses to beauty and right." That is what my religion, Judaism, said three thousand years ago when it spoke of God, the spirit of the universe, the spirit of truth and righteousness, that He demands of His children loyalty to truth and righteousness, *imitatio dei,* following in the footsteps of the Father, however stumblingly.

Before that same bar of reason I test my other Jewish beliefs, beyond that of ethical monotheism, beyond the belief in a one God all good and all righteous. I find it reasonable to believe that God the merciful will judge us mercifully, and that to approach near unto Him, man needs no mediator. All that God desires from us, as the Jewish prophet long ago stated, is "to do justice, to love mercy and to walk humbly before God." And if we do — what does Judaism say will happen? Harps, and halos, a material heaven? Otherwise, an eternal fiery hell? Here my religion walks very warily, for it knows so little. It says nothing of heaven, the material heaven, or a fiery hell, but it has a very fervent hope of the immortality of the soul, to which it holds without speculating about the condition of that future life of the soul.

I am a Jew because so sound and sane and simple are the credos of Judaism, with no need to say "Credo quia absurdum est," I believe because it is absurd. There is nothing in Judaism that contradicts reason, no miracle upon which the structure of the faith in any way depends. It is a reasonable faith.

And I am a Jew because of the pragmatic reason that it is a faith that has been powerful enough to preserve the Jewish group throughout two thousand years, while it has been scattered abroad among the nations, with no land or other center, amid hate and persecution so fiery as to have burned away a million generations of men. Despised and rejected of men, the Jew has not sunk into the mire as all other rejected folks did, but upheld by his faith he has kept himself physically and spiritually clean, a virile, wholesome, stimulating, law-abiding group which still dreams dreams and sees visions and has enriched and is enriching mankind with the constantly evoked contributions of the spirit of Israel in every sphere of human living. I am a Jew because Israel, practically all the world over, is still sore bestead; for persecution, alas, is not exclusively a medieval phenomenon. I would consider it utterly despicable and cowardly to forsake my people in their extremity.

And lastly I am a Jew because I am proud of the history of my people and want to identify myself with that story to the end. With Whittier I could say:

> Who taught you tender Bible tales
> Of honey lands, of milk and wine?
> Of happy, peaceful Palestine?

Of Jordan's holy harvest vales?
Who gave the patient Christ? I say,
Who gave your Christian creed? Yea, yea!
Who gave your very God to you?
   Your Jew! Your Jew! Your hated Jew!

I am a Jew because of that history, because God chose
Israel to reveal Himself and His truth of righteousness
even as He chose the Greeks to reveal His truth of beauty
and the Romans to reveal His truth of law. I am a Jew
because I glory in the thought that it was the Jew who
gave mankind the Bible, the seers and psalmists and sages,
the eternal evidence of a people martyred yet steadfast
in the faith, patiently suffering and patiently blessing
those who tortured them. I am a Jew because I am proud
of Israel's past and sure of its destiny as the witness of
God in the earth, in the ages yet to be.